APOLOGETICS
FOR THE
REST OF US

A Beginner's Guide

By Ray Ciervo

No Pat Answers
c/o Ray Ciervo Ministries
PO Box 507
Oakhust, NJ 07755
www.NoPatAnswers.com

www.xulonpress.com

TABLE OF CONTENTS

Acknowledgements vii

Endorsements ix

Foreword xi

Introduction xiii

PART ONE

The Lay of the Land 23

Apologetics in the Scripture 33

The Truth about Truth 41

PART TWO

Tearing Down Strongholds 53

Always Be Ready 72

Contend 77

Common Ground 88

Certainty—Post Evangelism 97

PART THREE

Apologetics and Worldview 105

Arguments for God's Existence 112

The Problem of Evil 120

Conclusion 127
Recommended Resources 131
Endnotes 135
About Ray Ciervo 141

ACKNOWLEDGEMENTS

First and foremost I want to acknowledge my wife, Joanne, who has been my partner in ministry for nearly forty-one years. She has been my chief supporter, encourager, and consoler. Her resolute faith in God's call on my life continuously helped me make choices that served a greater purpose. This is not to say that she doesn't share in that calling—quite the contrary. This has been *our* calling together. Her encouragement to get this message in written format provided enough courage for me to take it on. I'm indebted to you, Joanne, for your faith and courage.

I also want to acknowledge my friend and pastor, Charles Simpson, for his support in my ministry and encouragement to study apologetics. He has never wavered in egging me on to finish my degree work or further study. He continues to be an integral part of our lives, and we are thankful for him and all he does.

Pastor Barry Wissler prompted me several times to write this message after hearing me preach and teach on apologetics. I'm thankful for Barry's persistence and his friendship over many, many years.

I have to thank two of my best friends while in seminary, David Mendez and Dr. Max Herrera. Both of them made me think about the concepts in this book and put them into simple language. David was always getting me to think about things differently. Max was a source of encouragement and patience explaining difficult concepts to my somewhat slow mind. Thanks guys!

Dr. Norman L. Geisler, and the faculty at Southern Evangelical Seminary, (2000-2002), in Matthews, North Carolina, provided an excellent education in apologetics, philosophy, and theology. I am grateful to have had the opportunity to study and learn so much from them.

There are many others who have supported me both financially and through their labors. Not least is Pastor Tony Moss of Long Branch Covenant Church, Long Branch, New Jersey, who has "opened the doors" to the church for me to practice my skill and art form. He and the congregation in Long Branch have welcomed Joanne and me to "do" apologetics in their house.

ENDORSEMENTS

There are many apologetics books on the market, but few like this volume which fits into a special niche. Like vacation brochures, it provides a sense of where you are going to travel and what may be available for you to experience. This book gives a perspective that orients the reader to the whole arena of apologetics in a fascinating way. It is interesting, readable, and a very helpful guide to a field every Christian has a divine duty to learn.

- Dr. Norman Geisler, PhD

Arriving just in time, Ray Ciervo's *Apologetics for the Rest of Us* is a much needed help to anyone engaging with our culture over the truth. Christianity must involve loving God with both our hearts and our minds. Since our faith is also rational, this book will help you! When we know the truth, we do not need to be defensive. This is a very readable book that will inform you and build your confidence for reaching the lost.

- Barry Wissler, (M.A.R.; WTS)
Sr. Pastor, Ephrata Community Church

The study of apologetics can make evangelism fun, but it seems to take a lot of heavy study to learn this subject. Ray's book is a wonderful introduction to apologetics that is readable by anyone, and whets the reader's appetite for more.

Ray makes the case why Christians need to defend their faith by grounding it in Scripture. He brings the subject of apologetics to the "rank and file" of the church with clear examples of why the subject is necessary and *doable*. The book is a clearly readable and compelling introduction to a subject too often shunned because of its complex language. We need more books like this to get the ordinary believers interested in a lifelong study of apologetics so they can win their family, friends, neighbors, and co-workers to Christ.

- *Rick Schenker, President—Ratio Christi*

We rely on evidence for important decisions in this temporary life. But what if our lives spill over into eternity? Wouldn't evidence be even more important? That's why you need to read *Apologetics for the Rest of Us* by my friend Ray Ciervo!

**- *Dr. Frank Turek, DMin.,*
*Founder and Director of CrossExamined.org***

FOREWORD

Apologetics for the Rest of Us is the book that I wish I had read prior to entering college. In my very first term at college, I sat under a geology professor who was an atheist and openly mocked faith in God. Of course, things have not gotten better in the ensuing years. Fortunately, I had a good biblical background, but often was unable to articulate my reasons or my defense of *the faith*. Unfortunately, I watched as other young people fell under the influence of atheism. If they did not outright deny the faith, their witness became muted.

We can be emotional about our faith, but emotions cannot answer the onslaught of questions that face us in the world, and therein lays a great problem for the church and its constituents. God does reach our emotions, but there must be a firm foundation of both reason and experience beneath our emotions. Too often churches fail to provide that foundation.

Sound apologetics give us a basis to answer the questions that are being asked, often by well-intended inquirers. We must soundly address their questions. As I read Ray's manuscript I began to think of others who would be helped by it, and went so far as to discuss it with a young non-Christian with whom I have been dialoging. He immediately expressed his desire to read the book. I believe that there is a vacuum that this book can fill in youth and adults alike.

Apologetics for the Rest of Us is not only good arguments for faith, but biblical arguments. It addresses the Apostle Peter's admonition to be ready to give a reason for the hope that is in us. It tells us how to demolish the strongholds that imprison so many minds in our time. The Gospel addresses both hearts and minds. We must do both.

Ray's effort does not assume that we already have a basic understanding of the subject. He takes us from a place of being unsure as to how to defend our belief in God, to a place of confidence and being able to take the offensive without giving offense. Ray gives the arguments without being argumentative. He allows the Truth to do its own work.

Like most ministers, I carry a burden for our culture that has been evangelized by secularism, postmodernism, and a host of other malignant influences. This is a tool that can be applied as a medicine for the mind that can search out false foundations and bring thoughts captive to Christ. It is worth more than one read, more than a few bites; it deserves a digestion that will nourish our faith.

I have known Ray Ciervo for many years and know his spiritual and mental acumen and his integrity. I therefore urge that his work be not only read and studied, but that we pass it on as good stewards of Truth and stewards our great salvation!

Charles Simpson, Pastor

INTRODUCTION

I paced up and down the hallway of my house; book in hand and a strained look on my face. As I mumbled to myself, my wife asked me what was the matter.

"I don't get it," I answered. "I know every word in the paragraph, but I don't know what the author is saying."

My wife looked on sympathetically.

"You'll get it. You're smart," she offered.

Smart? I thought. "Smart doesn't have anything to do with this. Don't you understand? I know all the words, but I have no idea what he's talking about!"

The book was a Penguin Classic, *Selected Writings of Thomas Aquinas*. Recently, we had moved away from New Jersey where I had pastored for three years. As I faced some new challenges in my own life and wrestled with where I thought the world was going, I had begun to study apologetics. With my wife Joanne's support, I began to look for courses that taught apologetics. That led me to a seminary and a move to just outside of Charlotte, North Carolina, where I was enrolled at Southern Evangelical Seminary.

I jumped in with both feet. At age fifty-two I didn't believe I had the opportunity to take the scenic route and stretch the program out to four or five years. No, I was going to do this in the minimum amount of time. First semester was a full load. I was taking four courses which included hermeneutics, introduction to ancient philosophy, prolegomena, and great thinkers like Thomas Aquinas. Yes, Thomas Aquinas.

I'd heard of Aquinas, maybe even read some quotes by him. However, existence and essence, act and potency, and a few of his other concepts had me beyond perplexed. I wanted to give up, throw in the towel, and go home. I apologized to my wife for moving her and our two Australian shepherds from the safety of our familiar home to a new place where we knew few people. Over and over Joanne extended sympathy and gently reassured me that I would get it. Did she know something I didn't?

This was the big league and I felt like I was striking out. I was frustrated. I often thought of giving up. *What did I get us into?* I wondered. However, I knew quitting wasn't an option, and with Joanne's daily encouragement, I pressed on. It was the right thing to do. The way I saw it, there was a lot at stake. It wasn't about my pride, but about the future of our world.

I had been involved in church ministry as a pastor, church planter, and conference speaker. I had trained leaders and led a network of churches. I had read so many books on church leadership I could anticipate the next point an author would make. I'd read theology and wrestled through some of the finer points so I was no stranger to research or study, but until now it had come pretty easy to me. This, however, was heavy lifting.

Despite the difficulty, I persisted until I gained a full understanding of the subject. Apologetics can be a daunting subject; however, it is also intriguing. People who see the need for apologetics can sometimes, like I did, feel frustrated by the lack of accessible material. I have read many books more than once to understand what I was reading. Only persistence and a continual personal urging to understand this subject kept me going. It was not an easy task, but it was well worth the effort.

Now, I am writing this book as an accessible introduction to apologetics. If this is your first book on apologetics,

I trust it will not be your last. As I began to study apologetics in seminary, I recognized the need for a "gateway book" on the subject that would provide information in easy-to-read language. Thus, this book is intended as a starting point that will compel you to progress toward more in-depth study. I believe you will find this book both accessible and rewarding. If you become gripped by the importance of apologetics, I am confident you will buy many more books on it.

Many who have attempted to understand apologetics have ended up discouraged by the depth and density of many books on the subject. However, *Apologetics for the Rest of Us,* as the title indicates, is different. It is not meant to be deep nor profound. It is simply to introduce you to some of the basics, and ground you in some of the scriptures related to apologetics.

Apologists study long and hard. They tackle subjects like philosophy, theology, history, science, and logic. Not everyone has the time (or the motivation) to become an apologist. However, *apologetics* is a necessary study for every believer. We are not all called to be professional apologists, but we all need to learn to defend our faith. That is why this is *apologetics for the rest of us.*

We must all know what we believe and be able to give reasons for why we do. Even those who say they don't believe in anything (which is, itself, a belief) ought to have a reason for their stance. Buddhists, Hindus, atheists, and followers of each of the world religions and belief systems should have clear reasons for their beliefs (or lack of them). It is reported that Socrates, the great Greek philosopher, said, "The unexamined life is not worth living."

"Just Follow Your Star"

I once spoke to someone who told me, "You just have to follow your star."

I was intrigued. As I questioned her about what she meant, it was immediately apparent that she didn't know. She had intended to say something profound, but when I asked her to explain, she fumbled for clarity and ended up telling me she'd have to think more about it. She didn't have a clear understanding or explanation for the philosophy that was guiding her life.

I imagine her saying meant something like, "Go with the flow" or "Follow the rhythms of life." These commonly-used phrases are really nonsensical statements that are, at best, fatalistic. They lack direction and meaning; they don't go anywhere. This may seem silly to us as believers, yet unfortunately many Christians who claim Jesus as their Lord and Savior adopt a similar sort of stance. They don't know very well *what* they believe, and even fewer know *why* they believe it. Sadly, all too often the explanations people give for their belief in Christ also sound nonsensical and are difficult for unbelievers to understand or relate to.

These nonsensical responses are known as *pat answers*. Common Christian pat answers are, "It's in the Bible," or "The Bible says...." A pat answer—a trite, glib, and poorly thought-out response communicates a defensive posture that says, "Leave me alone." Like the woman's advice to "follow my star," these are superficial responses that we too often substitute for meaningful and intelligent explanations.

This should not be the way we reflect the gospel to the world. Rather, we must know not only what we believe but why. Then we'll be able to make a defense to everyone who asks us to give a reason for the hope within our hearts (see 1 Peter 3:15). Sadly, for many believers particularly in the United States this is not the case. We must make a change!

Of course, this isn't just an individual problem. It relates to the way we do church as a culture. Though some churches do place a strong emphasis on doctrine and expository preaching, in most evangelical churches doctrine and apologetics are underplayed or ignored. Instead, sermons focus on topical stories or current events that relate loosely to biblical ideas. Considering this, it would not be completely wrong to say that the evangelical church in the United States is anemic. In many cases, it appears that the world has done a better job of influencing the Church rather than the other way around.

Because of this, we are currently losing the battle for ideas. This affects every other area of life, including morality, education, family, politics, and many others. It's easy to look at a particular social issue—like the removal of prayer from public schools—and think that is the problem. However, the truth is that it's a symptom of a deeper problem—*our inability to defend our faith.*

The Massive Implications

For example, let's talk about Darwinism or Neo-Darwinism[1] which has become our society's default explanation for how life flourished on the earth. The inability of Christians to effectively defend the Bible has resulted in the rise of Darwinism, not just in biology but also in psychology and ethics. Though it originated as an explanation for biological life, Darwinism has become the explanation of life itself. According to this belief system we can have life without God. Darwinism promotes the idea of *naturalism*. Naturalism claims that the physical world is all that is real. There is no mind, no spirit, and no soul. Technically, this is called *metaphysical naturalism* or more simply *philosophical naturalism*. In a nutshell, it teaches that the only things that are real are what our five senses can assimilate or comprehend.

It is not difficult to see this is an unsustainable view of life. The message of the gospel and the knowledge that God does exist encourages us to tackle these ideas. Even if we have been unsuccessful in the past, we have no reason to believe we will never be successful. In fact, we see Neo-Darwinism crumbling in many areas.[2]

Philosophical Naturalism (PN) teaches that only what your senses can take in is real. If PN is true then Christianity is false. They make opposite claims about reality. (I'll talk more about naturalism later.) According to the Bible, God is Spirit and humans are living souls; both of which PN denies. Hard core naturalists would even say we don't have a free will. In the end, our minds are simply firing neurons and molecules in motion.

I know *that* sounds simplistic. A sophisticated description is that our actions are not the result of free will, but that we respond to antecedent causal circumstances. In other words, we are hardwired to react with no choice involved. Darwinian thought gives rise to this as well.

PN has also given other ideas like relativism a place to flourish. Though it may seem strange that a "hard" science like biology can influence "soft" sciences like sociology, psychology and history, the reality is that when Darwin offered "life without God," it impacted everything. If biology could prove God doesn't exist, then everything is permissible. If there is no God, then there is no truth or hope for a principled moral society—at least not as the Bible describes morality. This is a bit ironic as relativism and naturalism (supported by Darwinism) are ideological opposites. In short, the irony is that relativism declares there are no absolutes, and naturalism depends on absolutes.

The effect of Darwinism on the social sciences might not seem obvious, but it is very real. Take psychology, for example. Evolutionary psychologists have actually made excuses for rapists saying they have a gene that was once needed for procreation (as if rape was the only way men and women formed unions). Because a man had to force himself on a woman at one time many, many years ago, this gene sometimes shows up in modern men, who then become rapists. It's not his fault that he rapes, they argue.[3] The same thing has been said about serial murderers.[4] Through these arguments, Neo-Darwinian thought has attempted to excuse any accountability or responsibility on the part of the perpetrator.

Bioethics, a relatively new discipline, is another example. Those who study bioethics essentially determine who lives and who dies, where medical expenses get paid, and who is refused medical expenses. All of it is based on whether or not someone will continue to produce for society. In this way, ethics has relied on Darwin's theories to determine who will help the human race progress. Those who show little chance of helping our forward progress are no longer useful to society. Thus, they find themselves wanting for medical attention.

Looking at just these few examples, it is easy to see that we're in a battle of ideas. As the Church, we are in danger of losing. Thus far the result has been an amorally relative society where the present culture decides right and wrong, and the academy denies the role of absolute truth in discerning true and false.

Thus pluralism, same-sex marriage, and pre-marital sex are increasingly accepted while any restriction on human behavior has been cast off to Taboo-Land. A Bible-believing Christian literally cannot discuss these issues without being called a "bigot," "a homophobe" or "an idiot."

When you see the reality of the battle we're in, it is easy to see the necessity of apologetics. You will also begin to realize how important it is if you become engaged in the conversation and find yourself lacking the proper training to interact on an intellectual level.

Apologetics for the Rest of Us will help to the open the door, and get you started on the journey toward being able to intelligently and effectively defend your faith.

PART ONE

Chapter One

THE LAY OF THE LAND

I felt about as helpless as a fish without fins. I am a Vietnam Vet so the feelings of uneasiness and helplessness were not new to me. However, I wasn't in a war zone—at least not one that I recognized. I was across the table from a young college student, and I found myself with little to say.

The college student was someone I knew, someone I had known for a long time. In fact, I had known him from his childhood, and had watched him grow and develop a relationship with the Lord. Now he was asking me questions to which I had no answers. I realized he was thinking of jettisoning his faith in favor of atheism if he didn't get reasonable answers. I had none. He questioned the reliability of the New Testament documents, biological evolution, and absolute morals. Admittedly, I was stumped. My first reaction was simply to say, "Just believe; you know Jesus is real." However, wisdom told me that would be the end of the conversation.

The only answer I could muster was, "I don't know how to answer these questions, but I'll tell you what, I'll find answers to all of them."

This situation was one of many used by God to get me to study apologetics. I have received calls, emails, and letters from parents asking and sometimes begging me for answers because their children were leaving their Christian beliefs behind. In many cases the sad response is this is going to be a tough fight. I have since learned I was in a war zone, only this was a battle for ideas. This is a battle for which many are not equipped, and far too many are clueless about the fight.

My desire to defend the historic Christian faith is matched only by my desire to build the Church of Jesus. As I mentioned in the Introduction, Christian apologetics or the defending of the historic Christian faith is a subject and discipline the Church sorely needs. As American Christians who believe in the essentials of Christianity[5] we find ourselves in hostile territory. These days, we cannot bring the name of Jesus into a conversation without facing mockery, disinterest or disbelieving questions about whether we really believe *that stuff*. Our culture has marginalized the Church making our influence trivial. According to trending opinions, our faith is only valid in a private setting and has no place in the public square.

If morality is discussed, the Christian view is not considered and Christians are held at arm's length. Society does not believe that the Christian Church has anything to offer by way of morality. As we have stated already, the default position is that Darwin was right and that life exists without God. If we want to believe in God, we are told to keep it to ourselves because society, not God, is the judge of what is acceptable and not acceptable. As a result, relativism, the idea that there are no absolute truths or morals ruling the world of conduct, has won the day. Few believe in universal right behaviors or a code of conduct anymore. Since we have no final authority, society has become the final authority that determines what is permissible.

A Word about Apologetics

Apologetics, like any other subject, does not exist in a vacuum. I have met well-meaning people who want to learn the discipline and art of apologetics for themselves. There is little intention, if any, to practice apologetics in any of the arenas available. What those people believe is that apologetics *does* exist in a vacuum, but this is not true. Apologetics cannot exist in a vacuum. This is true in at least two ways. The first way is that the study of apologetics is part of *evangelism*. Second, it is part of *rhetoric,* which is a manner of arguing, expressing a point or clearly presenting evidence to persuade. Let's look at these two more closely.

Some have called the use of apologetics *pre-evangelism* because it helps people see the truthfulness of the gospel of Jesus Christ. I refer to this as removing the mental obstacles that prevent people from considering the evidence for God's existence or the Resurrection. It is also *post-evangelism* in that the evidence given by apologetics helps to strengthen the believer's faith; they are comforted and bolstered by the reasons or proof for the validity of what they believe. I have watched people begin to smile as they grasp the evidence apologists can present for the truthfulness of the gospel. They are reassured that their faith is placed in solid facts.

Evangelism

In pre-evangelism, some have described apologetics as the means to removing mental obstacles that may prohibit people from considering the truth of Christianity. Others have described it as a vehicle that removes roadblocks on the road to salvation. People cannot reach the place of salvation with these roadblocks in place so apologetics help to get rid of the roadblocks. Another way to express this concept is that apologetics remove the camouflage. In this analogy, the camouflage is any idea that prohibits a person from seeing the truth of the gospel. As camouflage disguises animals or hunters, divergent ideas hide the truth of Jesus. Apologetics reveal the true nature of the gospel that has been hidden by so many divergent ideas. As pre-evangelism, apologetics prepare people to hear and consider the unique truthfulness of Jesus Christ, and allows the Holy Spirit to convict people concerning their lives.

As post-evangelism, apologetics strengthen believers. Doug Powell says, "The results of training in apologetics are boldness, security, and a lack of defensiveness. Apologetics enable the believer to engage the world without acquiescing to it and without compromise."[6]

According to Powell, knowing the evidence that supports Christianity emboldens believers and enables them to interact with the world in a secure (not defensive) manner. When challenges come and we are able to respond without being defensive, it begins to level the playing field. Removing the emotional element that so often results from being challenged causes the momentum of the argument to shift. We, as believers, are now able to frame[7] the argument, and present the solid evidence we have learned regarding the existence of God and the resurrection of Jesus without compromising our faith.

The ability to resist compromising one's faith is especially crucial for college students who live in an environment which is hostile to Christianity. It is true for any Christian who lives and works in an environment that may be hostile to Christianity. However, the college environment is especially hostile toward Christianity. When you are in college, you're in enemy territory. Day after day, college students hear what seems to be evidence against Christianity, as well as deriding comments about Christians and the history of the Church. Many struggle to keep their faith at these times—unless they are equipped with the unique truthfulness of the Christian faith.

26

In a later chapter, I explore the idea of certainty in knowing the exact truth. This is often overlooked as a necessary part of the Christian faith. We think that knowing prevents us from growing in faith. This is a serious problem. The truth is our minds are not stumbling blocks to our faith. In fact, what our hearts believe our minds seek to know and understand. It is true that we cannot know *everything* about God, but that doesn't mean we cannot know *anything* about God. Personally, I want to know as much as I can and seek the wisdom and knowledge God. As wise Solomon wrote, "Then you will discern the fear of the LORD and discover the knowledge of God. For the LORD gives wisdom; from His mouth come knowledge and understanding" (Proverbs 2:5-6). Finding evidence for my faith only strengthens it.

Admittedly, it's not just the Church that has become anti-intellectual. American culture in general has placed a decreasing value on diligent study and thorough knowledge. Consider this quote:

> *Rhetoric faded in academia during the 1800s, when social scientists dismissed the notion that an individual could stand up to the inexorable forces of history. Who wants to teach leadership when academia doesn't believe in leaders? At the same time, English lit replaced the classics, and ancient thought fell out of vogue. Nonetheless, a few remarkable people continued to study the art. Daniel Webster picked up rhetoric at Dartmouth by joining a debating society, the United Fraternity, which had an impressive classical library and held weekly debates. Years later, the club changed its name to Alpha Delta and partied its way to immortality by inspiring the movie Animal House.[8]*

This is an extreme example, but it touches on the course of education in America. The classics have been replaced, and rhetoric has been abandoned at the behest of social scientists. We'll talk more about this later, but for now let's look at the importance of rhetorical skills and how they relate to apologetics.

Rhetorical Skills

The second companion to apologetics is rhetoric, which is a way of speaking. *Rhetoric* as a term has been hijacked and given a pejorative meaning that wasn't part of the original definition. Thus to many, *rhetoric* is a style of speaking that twists truths and gives snide responses. The term is also used to demean someone's argument. "That's rhetoric," is heard when someone doesn't like a rehearsed position. In fact it may be rhetoric, but that doesn't make it bad. As I mentioned the term has been hijacked. In reality, rhetoric is a style of arguing designed to convince other people to change their position.

We find a good example of this in Acts 17:1–4, where we discover that it was Paul's custom to go to the synagogue and reason with the Jews, explaining and giving evidence that Jesus was the Christ. Although Paul did this from the Scriptures, he was employing rhetorical skills that would have convinced those particular Jews who were born in the Greek culture. By birth they were Jews, but by culture they were Greek! They understood Greek thinking, Greek language, and Greek rhetoric. They are the Hellenist Jews of Acts 7. Knowing this, Paul "reasoned with them from the Scriptures, explaining and giving evidence that the Christ had to suffer and rise again from the dead..." (Acts 17:2–3). In verse four, we see that some of them were *persuaded* and joined Paul and Silas.

It is no accident that Luke used the word *persuaded* in conjunction with *reasoned, explaining,* and *giving evidence.* This is rhetoric at its finest. Paul moved these Jews to see his point and change their beliefs. Paul was doing the work of an apologist, defending the faith by using rhetorical skills. Thus we see that apologetics reside within the realm of rhetoric, which unfortunately is something the Church knows far too little about. That, of course, is one of the purposes of this book. Let's step up to the plate to learn.

Apologetics, Apologetic, and Apologists

Before we go too much farther, however, we need to clarify some terminology. Terms such as *apologist, apologetic,* and *apologetics* are new to many believers. They sound a lot like *apology* which is what we say when we are sorry for something. Certainly, we are not saying we are sorry we are Christians!

Those who are familiar with the word *apologetics,* unfortunately, often think of it as winning an argument or an ideological fight. While it is true that some people study apologetics to "make points" as if scoring more points than the opponent is winning, that is not the ultimate purpose of apologetics. As Americans, we live on one-liners. We love to believe that with a quick quip we can shut the opponent down. This is not Christian apologetics. Winning arguments and losing friends (or potential converts) is devastating to the Christian message, and it is not representative of Christian apologetics.

My apologetic ministry sponsors seminars called *No Pat Answers.* A pat answer is a trite, glib shot from the hip that is not well thought out. For those who inquire about the Christian faith or those who argue with the basic beliefs of the Christian faith, there ought to be no pat answers. Our answers must be clear, cogent, and compelling responses. We must learn what apologetics are before we can harness the strength of this art form.

Apologia, the Greek word we derive our word *apology* from means "a defense." Paul helps us to understand that with his usage of the word in Acts 22:1, *"Brethren and fathers, hear my defense...."* The word for "defense" is *apologia.* This refers to a defense in the legal sense, as a lawyer would use in a court of law. It is not a military defense. When Peter tells us to always be ready "to make a defense to everyone who asks you to give an account for the hope that is in you," he also tells us to do it with "gentleness and reverence" (1 Peter 3:15). The emphasis on making a defense is tempered by gentleness and reverence. In other words, the attitude of the apologist must take the listener into account. *Gentleness* is strength under control, and *reverence* is respect for the people we talk to. Apologetics are not about winning arguments and making the other person look bad. In the context of rhetoric, it is about winning people over or moving people to see our position in a favorable light. Thus, we can adopt the motto: Argue without being argumentative, and defend without being defensive.

Too many believers are turned off by apologists who seek only to win an argument by points, or worse to show off how much they know. I was once spending time with a young college professor who held some pretty lofty ideas about religion. He'd studied abroad and was well versed in Hinduism and Buddhism. I had spent weeks meeting with him over coffee at a local coffee shop discussing different ways we know the truth claims of his religions and of course mine.

One morning after we finished a discussion over coffee, we were getting ready to leave when a young man interrupted us and began to tell my friend where he was wrong. Immediately, I knew what was going to happen and abruptly stopped the young budding apologist. His zeal to pounce on my friend's argument could have cost me weeks of laying a foundation. I'm not sure of his motives, but it was clear he wanted to "win" the argument or help me win it. Instead, apologists ought to seek to win hearts *and* minds through the use of persuasion, explanation, and evidence.

In philosophy, *apology* is a rhetorical term that means "to move people, to persuade them, to help them change their view, and to understand and accept yours." When we are *apologizing,* we are giving an argument (another term that is too often misused and misunderstood). In rhetoric, as already stated, an argument is not a fight, it is not trying to score points, and it is not to put the other person down. It is persuading through reasonable statements, and offering evidence to prove our point and show our point's validity. Apologists "argue" in order to persuade, to move other people, and help them change their position. They should not argue to put other people down or simply win the argument. It is about hearts and minds. So the art of rhetoric is persuasion, and apologetics are at the heart of that art. *Apologia* is the legal defense, but it is used to persuade.

Make no mistake; apologists seek to make their defense strong, cogent, and persuasive. Remember, Peter denied Jesus at Jesus' trial, then cursed and swore when questioned about knowing Him (see Matthew 26:72-74). This same Peter tells us to always be ready to make a defense (*apologia*) to everyone who asks us to give a reason for the hope within our hearts, yet to do so with gentleness and reverence (see 1 Peter 3:15). Blustering, spontaneous Peter, who was remorseful for his earlier actions, reminds us to be gentle and reverent when we are making a defense. So apologists argue and seek to move people from an ignorant view of the Christian faith, to show that Christianity is reasonable, and move it into a more favorable position in their opponents' minds.

At one time, apologetics were not "the" sought after subject, and did not draw large crowds. It still does not

31

in some places, though the mood about apologetics is changing. Until recently, when I asked a congregation if anyone knew what I meant by apologetics, very few would respond in the affirmative. Now, more and more people are becoming aware of and are interested in apologetics. What was once reserved for the ivory tower of seminaries and higher education is now making its way to the water cooler, lunch table, and kitchen counter. It is becoming the interest of church-goers, Christian education teachers, and small groups. As a result, an increasing number of resources are becoming available through such stellar ministries as *Focus on the Family, Reasons to Believe, Faith and Reason, Ravi Zacharias International Ministries, Cross-Examined.org,* and many others. There are also many websites like YouTube and Vimeo Videos that can help to equip the believer in apologetics. These resources help to keep apologetics in a context and not in a vacuum that exists by itself. A good apologetic ministry understands both of the contexts of apologetics—the rhetorical and the evangelistic.

In summary, apologists are those who defend the historic Christian faith. This discipline or skill is called *apologetics.* There are many ways to defend our faith and several views on how apologetics ought to function. Those who use history support a historical apologetic. Others use science to defend their faith. Still others have a philosophical argument for apologetics. Then there are those who use all three—history, science, *and* philosophy.

At the end of the book, I've included a list of resource recommendations including books, websites, and videos. Hopefully, this will be your first book in a serious pursuit of apologetics.

Chapter Two

APOLOGETICS IN THE SCRIPTURE

My wife and I have moved our family more than a few times. Some of those times we have moved into "new" neighborhoods where we had to pick out a floor plan and wait for the house to be constructed. I would go to the building site from the earliest stages of construction and watch things come together. My wife would find it interesting that I would go to watch them dig the hole for the footing and foundations. I'm not sure why, but I was always interested in the foundation.

The first house we bought was about twenty-five years old. I had looked at over forty houses before I found the one we would buy. I was young and inexperienced in shopping for houses. I knew little, if anything, about buying a house as this was my first. I didn't know what to look for and what would become a problem. I needed someone more experienced. I brought my dad, who had a lot of experience, to help me make a decision on this first house.

One of the first things he did was take me in the basement and look at the foundation. I remember him folding his arms and smiling as he looked at a solid concrete foundation. Not concrete block, but poured concrete walls. From my dad's perspective, this was the best you could ask for.

"This is about as solid as you can get," he said to me. "It's a good choice."

From that time on, I became interested in the foundation of every house we had constructed. I wanted to know what kind of foundation it would be. Unfortunately, my first house was the last for a poured concrete foundation. Most today are concrete block that are then filled with concrete. However, I would go and watch the builders dig the hole and pour the footings. Then the forms would be constructed. Foundations are extremely important.

For Christians to fully embrace apologetics, it is essential and foundational that we see that Christian apologetics are biblical because they have biblical usage and a biblical interpretation. First, it is crucial for the church to embrace apologetics. This subject is not meant to be an answer to everything, but a necessary tool in the church's equipment. In order for the church to do this willingly, it must accept this as biblical and not an arbitrary task.

First, let's look at the usage of the word for apologetics, *apologia,* in the New Testament. As already noted, *apologia* is the word used for "defense" in the New Testament. The New Testament was written in what is known as *Koine* Greek which was common Greek or the language of the Greeks spread throughout the larger Mediterranean as a trade language. It became such a common (*Koine*) trade language that even the Romans used it. It is not as sophisticated as classical Greek, but it was definitely used more extensively. It was the more common trade language.

Like much of the *Koine* Greek used in New Testament times, *apologia* finds usage in Classical Greek first. Perhaps it was Plato who popularized the term in his *Apology,* Socrates' defense. Socrates, who was Plato's mentor, was accused of corrupting young people, refusing to worship the gods, and promoting "new" gods. Plato's *Apology* is Socrates' defense of his actions at his trial. In this context, we can see the legal aspect of this term as we discussed in Chapter One. Thus, we can safely say that in the biblical sense, apologizing is to give a defense for our faith.

In the last chapter, we talked about the context of apologetics which is important for understanding its New Testament usage. When we understand that apologetics are used in the context of rhetoric and evangelism, we see that it is also about being proactive. Thus, it is about persuading through evidence. This is important to keep in mind as we look at the scriptures that use the word *apologia* or demonstrate the actions of apologetics.

Luke, Paul, and Peter all use *apologia* in their writings. Luke quotes Paul's use of the word in Acts 22 and 25. Both times Luke quotes Paul using the term to describe his "apology" for his actions. In Acts 22:1, Paul is accused of bringing Gentiles into the temple. When seized by Roman guards, he asks to speak to the people and begins by saying, "Brethren and fathers, hear my defense [apologia] which I now offer to you." Clearly, Paul intended to defend his actions.

Similarly, in Acts 25 Paul is brought before Festus, the Roman Governor of Judea. Explaining why he is there, Paul recites Roman law about the accused having the right to face his accuser and then goes on to say, "... and has an opportunity to make his defense [apologia] against the charges" (Acts 25:16). Again it is clear that Paul intended to state his reasons for his actions. Paul was seeking to move his listeners from an unfavorable position toward him to a favorable one.

Paul also uses the term several places in his letters. In 1 Corinthians 9:3, Paul states, "My defense [apologia] to those who examine me is this." Also in 2 Corinthians 7:11, Paul uses *apologia* to applaud the Corinthians' behavior. Here the word *apologia* is translated "vindication" which could be a successful apology. In 2 Timothy 4:16 Paul refers to another formal trial he was in saying, "At my first defense...." Here again *apologia* is used in a courtroom as a legal term. In this case, it is the whole trial that is Paul's defense.

In Philippians Paul uses *apologia* twice in direct reference to the gospel. First, Paul expresses his love for the Philippian believers because they are with him in partaking of the grace of God in his imprisonment, and for the confirmation and defense of the gospel (see Philippians 1:7). We will discuss this idea of *confirmation of the gospel* in a later section. In this case, Paul is referring to his ministry. He was called to both confirm and defend the gospel.

Later in the same chapter, Paul declares, "...I am appointed for the defense of the gospel" (Philippians 1:16). Paul understood that the world is hostile territory, and that ministry involves defending the gospel. This was not a light statement. His appointment was to defend the gospel because of the challenges that faced it in his day. Today, this challenge is no less, and the need for individuals to know they are appointed for the defense of the gospel may be even greater.

Probably the best-known verse concerning apologetics is found in 1 Peter 3:15. Here Peter uses the term in the context of sharing our faith by giving a reason for the hope within our hearts:

> *Sanctify Christ as Lord in your hearts, always being ready to make a defense to everyone who asks you to give an account for the hope that is in you, yet with gentleness and reverence.*

The context of this verse is based upon trials and perhaps persecution. Thus, Peter tells us how Christians should respond to such adversity. First he says, "Sanctify Christ as Lord in your hearts." This means acknowledging Christ's lordship in our lives. The heart has many functions ascribed to it, but in Peter's reference it most likely means "the center of our being." It refers to our true selves; who we really are as opposed to what we may want people to believe about us. Peter is exhorting his readers to settle down and get a grip on Christ being Lord of their lives. Sometimes it ought to be a daily exercise, and at other times it is a moment by moment revelation. Sanctifying Christ as Lord means acknowledging that He is the ruler of the universe, the King of kings, and the Lord of lords. More than that, He is our Lord—*your Lord*. We must bow to Him outwardly and inwardly.

Secondly Peter emphasizes, "Always being ready...." Readiness is an important aspect of this command, which we will discuss in a later chapter in this book. For now let's focus on the third part—"make a defense to everyone...." Peter's exhortation to be ready with a defense cannot be understated. The way to be ready is to know what you believe and why you believe it.

Having reasons for our faith is a necessity. These reasons include our personal experiences as well as the objective truth about God—including His character, the resurrection of Christ, and His immanence in our lives. These are all reasons for the hope within. Each of us must know not only *what* we believe, but *why* we believe it. And this requires some investigation, research, and study. Make no mistake; this is hard work, but it is very important work, too.

Remembering that defense indicates a legal defense, we see that Peter is referring to giving reasons for the hope within, and giving reasonable accounts for why we are not troubled as others are when we encounter trials. We need to be prepared when these questions are asked:

"How do you know Jesus is alive?"

"How do you know God exists?"

"How do you know God is with you?"

We can answer, "My faith rests on personal confirmation, philosophical, historical, scientific, and archeological evidence."

It is reasonable to affirm faith in God when there is so much evidence for Him.

Another way *apologia* is used is in the negative sense. In <u>Romans 1:20</u> Paul writes, "For since the creation of the world His invisible attributes, His eternal power and divine nature, have been clearly seen, being understood through what has been made, so that they are without excuse" (NASB).

Here the NASB translates *anapologia* as "without excuse." There is no defense for the actions of those who have clearly seen God's invisible attributes, eternal power, and divine nature. They are without an apology or a defense. God made Himself known to people through their conscience and their knowledge of reality, but they have suppressed this truth in unrighteousness. When it is God who provides the evidence and the hearts of people are unwilling to recognize it, they are without excuse. They have no argument, no apology.

About this, Craig Keener writes this:

> *Stoic philosophers argued that the nature of God was evident in creation; Cicero at that time could even assert that no race of humanity was so uncivilized as to deny the existence of the gods, and along with others he argued that the human mind points to what God is like.*
>
> *Jewish people scattered throughout the Greco-Roman world used this argument to persuade pagans to turn to the true God. Even the rabbis tell delightful stories about*

*how Abraham reasoned back to the first
cause and showed his fellow Gentiles that
there was really only one true God. According
to Jewish tradition, God had given seven
laws to Noah, for which all humanity was
responsible (including the prohibition of idol-
atry). But unlike Israel, who had to keep all
613 commandments in the law (according
to rabbinic count), most Gentiles disobeyed
even the seven laws of Noah.*[9]

Keener's point here is that when Paul wrote this, he
wasn't saying something new about unbelievers. It was
commonly accepted that both Jews and Gentiles had
this knowledge of God as revealed in creation. However,
some chose to suppress the truth in unrighteousness.
Therefore, they were without a defense.

Another passage often quoted by apologists is found
in 2 Corinthians 10:3–5

*For though we walk in the flesh, we do not
war according to the flesh, for the weapons of
our warfare are not of the flesh, but divinely
powerful for the destruction of fortresses.
We are destroying speculations and every
lofty thing raised up against the knowledge
of God, and we are taking every thought
captive to the obedience of Christ.*

Although the word *apologia* is nowhere in the text,
the fact that this is an apologetic text cannot be denied.
Here Paul describes his ministry as tearing down fortresses and every lofty thing that is raised against the
knowledge of God.

Similarly, in Titus 1:9 Paul wrote Titus to exhort the
elders by saying, "Holding fast the faithful word which is
in accordance with the teaching, so that he will be able

both to exhort in sound doctrine and to refute those who contradict."

In Colossians 4:6 he commands the believer, "Let your speech always be gracious, seasoned with salt, so that you may know how you ought to answer each person." Here Paul is commanding believers to be gracious *so that* they will know how to answer each person.

Clearly Paul used apologetics in his ministry. What about Jesus? Did He practice apologetics? In Scripture we can see that without question, Jesus also practiced apologetics. Norman L. Geisler and Patrick Zukerian write this:

> *Those who oppose apologetics in favor of a leap of faith without evidence will be disappointed in Jesus. Nowhere does he call on anyone to make an unthoughtful and unreasoned decision about his or her eternal destiny. Everywhere Jesus demonstrates a willingness to provide evidence for what he taught to every sincere seeker.*[10]

Jesus almost always gave evidence either from the Scripture or through miracles when He made claims about His role as Messiah. As Geisler and Zukerian wrote, Jesus didn't expect anyone to have blind faith. He presented evidence for the claims he made about himself. Jesus gave many defenses without becoming defensive. We are called to do the same.

Clearly in the passages we've perused in this chapter, we can see that apologetics played a significant role in the New Testament understanding of faith and evangelism. The New Testament appears to be written in anticipation of objections. Apologetic thinking was an integral part of the New Testament writings. May we apply that same understanding to our own day!

Chapter Three

THE TRUTH ABOUT TRUTH

It is difficult to ignore the truth. At least for me it is! Returning home from Vietnam in April of 1970 presented many problems for me and the truth. I had changed from the boy who went off to serve his country into someone who was somewhat skeptical and radical. To say I was confused would be an understatement. I had more questions than anyone could answer. Some said I had become a "street corner philosopher." Certainly I was thinking about current issues. Also, I was despairing because I didn't have answers.

I wouldn't describe my childhood as idyllic, but neither would I change very much. I had a good family life. My mother was a "stay at home mom," and rarely did I come home to an empty house. My dad was a hard-working cab driver who left the house before I woke up and returned at dinner time. In the 1950s, America was a good place to live. Even though I grew up in Brooklyn, New York, there's little I would change. Nothing much was out of harmony. When I tell people there were farms in Brooklyn when I was a boy, they look at me in disbelief. Honestly, there were farms.

However the sixties, as they've come to be known, changed all of that. The innocence of the fifties was gone. Music had begun to change even before the British invasion. The civil rights movement was front and center on TV as Black Americans demonstrated for equal rights and were met with water cannons and German shepherds. Then there was the "war" that was never officially declared. I'd been raised on WWII war movies where we were always the good guys. After encountering the real thing up close and personal, I experienced some changes.

I spent fifteen months on the only South Vietnamese Air Force Base in Vietnam. Most U. S. Air Force personnel lived in air conditioned quarters with high security fences protecting U.S. aircraft. Not me. I was one of a small contingent of Americans working on Binh Thuy Air Base in the Mekong Delta. We were there to support the South Vietnamese and train them to use our equipment. At times we were prohibited from leaving our base because "Charlie," the name given to the Viet Cong, was in town.

Before I go on with this story, let me say that I have the highest appreciation for the American soldier. Today I thank everyone I see in a military uniform when I have the opportunity to do so. However, in Vietnam the system failed the soldier and caused many to believe they were unsupported and in some ways forgotten. Many things that were told to the American public were not true. Many American serviceman felt disconnected from home and life itself. I was one of them.

I was discharged at Travis Air Force Base in California. I had been away from home for those fifteen months with few phone calls. To say I was anxious to get home would be an understatement. I hopped an overnight flight to JFK and landed sometime early the next morning. One of the first people I met had a look of disdain for my uniform. I wasn't shocked as I'd been told this was usually the response. This was just the beginning.

Months of failed adjustment to my civilian life left me cynical of many things. This was evident in a discussion of the politics of the war that I had with my father and an uncle. We talked about bombing civilians, body counts, and the kind of weapons that were used. Then our conversation went from the politics of the war to the protests at home. It was clear that my father and uncle thought I was very confused or even brainwashed because I questioned the government's policies. Surely we were living in trying times.

Through the conversation, both of them were attempting to "reach" me. They didn't know I was seeking deeper answers. One question led to another until finally I asked questions about reality: What is it all about? Who can you trust? How do you know what is true? Both of them just stared at me. Neither of them knew the answer, and it appeared as if neither of them had ever even sought the answer. The conversation was over. My last words at that time were about going to seek the truth.

The Church has not paid a lot of attention to truth. I'm not talking about the gospel, but about the idea of truth. Of course, when Paul says that the Church is *"the pillar and support of the truth"* (1 Timothy 3:15), he is referring to the gospel of Jesus Christ. However, the gospel is only true if it corresponds to reality which means this concept of truth must logically precede the gospel. In other words, the gospel of Jesus Christ is true *if* the proclamation of Jesus' life, death, and resurrection are in fact actual events. If Jesus never existed, then the gospel is not true. If Jesus was not crucified, then the gospel is not true. Even Paul agrees with this assessment when he says that if Christ did not rise from the dead, we among all people should be most pitied (see 1 Corinthians 15:19). This is because we would be believing and declaring something to be true that wasn't real.

It may help to define *reality*. What I mean by *reality* is "that which exists." A philosopher might define it as

43

"that which has 'being'." In other words, it is actual, not imaginary, and not simply living in the world of possibilities. Reality is something that actually exists.

The Truth and the Gospel

The truth is logical prior to the gospel because the gospel depends on the truth to be effective. The gospel claims are true if they correspond to actual events. This is the correspondent theory of truth. This "correspondence theory" of truth is the default position for truth. Ironically, even those who deny the reality of truth rely on the concept that truth exists. If truth did not exist, they could not make their claims. When people say, "There is no such thing as truth," they are making a self-defeating truth claim. Whenever people try to deny the truth, its objectivity or its absoluteness, they *must* affirm it. This may sound confusing; we will cover more on this later.

As the "pillar and support" of the truth, the Church has not done well in its role. This is true especially of the evangelical Church in twenty-first century America. As the pillar and support, the Church is not only to guard the gospel, but it is to guard truth. Without the underpinning of absolute truth, the truth of the gospel is ineffective. If Jesus is just another way to absolve a personal quest, then the truth of the gospel is useless. The claims of the New Testament declare Jesus to be alive from the dead and Lord of *all*. Either that claim is true or we are liars deceiving the masses.

Truth is always the first casualty in the battle for ideas. Dr. Geisler and Dr. Turek place the idea that truth exists and truth is knowable at the beginning of their excellent book, *I Don't Have Enough Faith to Be an Atheist*.[11] The book details twelve steps that show Christianity to be true. This is the classical approach to apologetics. First stop: *Truth*.

Absolutely Truth

An analogy will help here. Remember when you were taught to button your shirt or your blouse? The first button had to be inserted into the correct corresponding buttonhole. If it wasn't, it didn't matter how you tried to get the shirt or blouse to look right; it was always wrong. Now, there is no guarantee that if you button the first one right the others will all be right. You can still mess up down the row. However, getting the first button right gives you a better chance of getting the others right, too. The same is true for the truth. Getting the first one right doesn't guarantee you will get everything else right, but it does give you a way to measure or guide your understanding. This is why, when we are arguing for the truth of the gospel or God's existence, we must always defend this idea of truth. Without it there is no way to come to any meaningful conclusions.

Sadly, our twenty-first century culture has denigrated (or outright rejected) absolute truth. In our culture, truth has been categorized as relative, unknowable, or non-existent. These three categories are strikingly similar. After all, if truth is relative we must ask: *Relative to what?* It has to relate to something, and if it is only relative to relative, then it is unknowable in itself because that is nonsense. It must be relative to an absolute.

Logically, the statement that the truth is unknowable relies on the truth and that the truth is unknowable. That means we know the fact that truth is unknowable to be true. Once again, in trying to deny the truth it is logically affirmed. The same is true when someone attempts to say that there is no such thing as truth or that truth does not exist. To make this claim, a person must rely on a true statement to suggest that truth does not exist. These sorts of logical contradictions happen a lot when the subject of absolute morals comes into a conversation.

For instance, when people say there are no moral absolutes, they are inferring that morals are relative. However, they have relied on an absolutely true statement to argue that there are no moral absolutes. They have also inferred that the only moral absolute is the one that states morals are relative. We again call this a self-defeating statement. It is self-negating.

By declaring that no absolute morals exist, such people have made an absolutely moral statement. How? In essence, they have said it is wrong to believe in moral absolutes. Is that morally wrong or epistemologically wrong? (*Epistemology* is the science of knowing. It looks at how we know what we know.) The person who says it is wrong to believe in moral absolutes is wrong on both counts. At the very least, they are implying that it is morally wrong to say there are moral absolutes. Surely they are also saying it is epistemologically wrong to say there are such things as moral absolutes.

So the relativist who says, "Truth is unknowable," or "I know moral absolutes do not exist," has committed intellectual suicide by a self-defeating idea. The idea of no moral absolutes is an absolute statement. The relativist is stating that it is *wrong* to have moral absolutes. If people say no one can know the truth, is that a truth that they know? Don't they know that you cannot know? Once again, they have committed intellectual suicide by using a self-defeating statement.

Here's the truth about truth: We cannot deny the truth without using it. Try it. Whether we are talking about knowing the truth or the truth about moral absolutes, we cannot deny either without using them. To make a declaration that denies moral absolutes, we must make an absolute moral declaration. In other words, we are saying, "It is always wrong to make moral declarations." The person who says this is usually insinuating that it is morally wrong to do so.

Clearly, there is a lot of misunderstanding about the truth. Much of it pertains to the difference between the *concept* of truth and the *content* of truth. If the Church is the guardian of truth, it must at least be aware of the difference between them. For instance, Jesus said, "I am the way, and the truth, and the life..." (John 14:6). When Jesus said this was He claiming to be the definition of truth? Is truth a person? If so, that would mean that "Jesus" is the answer to every question because the right answer to every question is the truth. Clearly, this doesn't hold true. If we ask, "What color is the sky?" the right answer is not "Jesus." This is the difference between the concept of truth and the content of truth.

When Jesus said, "I am the truth," He was saying He is the content of the truth as it pertains to the Promised One of the Old Testament prophets. He is the only way to God the Father. Clearly, He is the content of that truth. Is He the promised Messiah? Yes, He corresponds to that truth. Is He the only way to the Father? Yes, again. He corresponds to these statements and fulfills the *content* of the answer. In this sense, He is the truth.

The *concept* of truth answers the question, "What defines the term *truth*?" The correspondence theory of truth answers that question. Truth is that which corresponds to what is real with respect to the time and sense of the statement. The sun is shining outside right now in Eatontown, New Jersey. This is true if and only if the sun is shining right now in Eatontown, New Jersey.

Truth does not depend on the character of the person speaking it. Likewise, my belief in the facts does not make something true. Truth exists whether I believe it or not. In that case, it is objective. Truth does not need me to know it in order for it to exist. Newton did not create the law of gravitation; he discovered it. This is the same as truth. We do not create it, we discover it. We do not construct it with our language either which is the declaration of postmodernists.

Postmodernists ascribe to the idea that the age of modernism is dying or already dead. As modernism promoted humanity's ability to reason their way to truth, postmodernists reject that idea. In fact, postmodernists reject any idea of knowing truth. Postmodernists generally do not believe truth exists as an absolute, but is constructed in our culture. Postmodernist philosophers attack different areas of modernist thinking such as language, truth, and reasoning. For the postmodernist there is no absolute meaning to anything except for what the individual gives to it. So truth is constructed not discovered.

Doug Groothuis says it this way:

> *...some claim that the whole modernist world has fallen apart and that we are held fast by nothing certain, nothing objective, nothing absolute, nothing universal. There is no finally fixed point of reference, no immovable anchor for the soul. We have entered post-modernity; the modernist ways of thinking about truth are impossible. Postmodernism, broadly understood, has dispensed with Truth and has replaced it with truths.*[12]

Of course, what postmodernists fail to realize is that they must be asked whether their statement about constructing truth was constructed. We rely on meaning and absolute meaning to understand just about everything. Making things up does not make sense, and it certainly does not make something true nor does it make it real.

Postmodernists will also make the statement that culture is trapped within its language and cannot speak outside of itself. One must look closely again and see that that statement, in order to be true, must also be trapped in its own language. Therefore, it cannot relate to anything outside of the culture of the person making it. Of course, what postmodernists mean is that *their* language is not trapped—just everyone else's.

For the Church to engage the culture it must dig into truth, understand it in its correspondence view, and apply it to its own theology and worldview. It must put truth first and declare that if Jesus Christ is not the person the New Testament declares Him to be, it must abandon its truth claims. This is why apologetics are so important. Apologetics provide the evidence for the uniqueness of Christ. Truth is always unique, narrow, piercing, and ultimately uplifting. Truth satisfies the heart when the mind questions. It builds confidence for the believer when the issues are settled. As Jesus told His followers, "If you continue in My word, then you are truly disciples of Mine; and you will know the truth, and the truth will make you free" (John 8:31-32).

PART TWO

Chapter Four

TEARING DOWN STRONGHOLDS

As a way of introducing the uninitiated to apologetics, I have on occasion preached a message using several scripture verses that illuminate the "how to" as well as some of the art of apologetics. I have found that this has helped many people's perspectives as they learn how to engage the culture. We have looked briefly at some of these verses already, but it's worth looking at them again.

First, let's look at 2 Corinthians 10:3-6:

> *For though we walk in the flesh, we do not war according to the flesh, for the weapons of our warfare are not of the flesh, but divinely powerful for the destruction of fortresses. We are destroying speculations and every lofty thing raised up against the knowledge of God, and we are taking every thought captive to the obedience of Christ, and we are ready to punish all disobedience, whenever your obedience is complete.*

Imagine going into a war with outdated weapons. This is what happened at the beginning of WWII.

Germany had secretly been developing not only strategy but tanks, airplanes, guns, and artillery that hadn't been used before. Most of Europe was still using WWI methods and weaponry. Poland still had horse cavalry that they tried to use as a defense against Germany's tanks. When Germany invaded Poland, they made short work of the Polish horse-soldiers.

Similarly, Germany had developed dive bombers and fighter planes while Poland used aircraft from WWI. Once again, the Germans made short work of the Polish Air Force. An army that was not ready and well equipped was easily over taken by one that was well equipped and well prepared.

Likewise, the fighting forces of the United States were not fit to fight the Japanese who attacked Pearl Harbor in December of 1941. The airplanes and ground soldiers were not up to fighting this new foe. The U.S. had to retool its armament and retrain it ground forces. The war in the Pacific was led largely by the U.S. Marine Corps. They had to retrain for jungle warfare and amphibious landings, and they had to learn to use new weapons. This new jungle warfare required new strategies as well as new weapons. If the U.S. was going to prevail, the fighting forces had to make adjustments.

Today the Church in twenty-first century America is in the same place. It *must* adjust to new conditions. First it is now in an environment that is hostile to the gospel. Second its equipment is outdated. What once worked for the Church does not work today, mainly because it does not recognize the kind of battle it is in. This is an ideological battle as well as spiritual warfare and the art of apologetics is a necessary tool for this battle. At one time the subject of apologetics was talked about more than used. One could say there wasn't much use for it. The culture was much friendlier to Christianity than it is today. However, all that has changed and the effect use of apologetics is necessary for today's church to succeed in its mission.

The study of apologetics is not an easy discipline or a light subject to study. That's why I've called it heavy lifting. However, the Church must realize that it is in a battle for ideas and that this battle is very important. This battle for ideas is a major challenge because ideas require thinking, and most people do not want to think about much. When I was in high school, I chose the path of least resistance for this very reason. That meant I picked the easiest subjects and those that required little work. Unfortunately, this is true of many people. We want quick answers or a place to find ready answers. We don't want to have to think about the answer. This is unfortunate because it leaves the Church without a way to judge good or bad arguments, let alone determine whether something is true or not. Apologetics provide the kind of weaponry needed to meet the challenge the Church faces.

The challenge facing the Church is the accusation that the Church is wrong—wrong in its beliefs about:

- God and the uniqueness of Jesus Christ
- the Bible
- its treatment of actions that were once considered sinful by society
- homosexuality
- same-sex marriage
- premarital sex
- morals in general

Today, the Church is believed to be wrong in its treatment of the poor, of science, of politics, of finances, of family life, and so forth. The list could go on and on.

So what is the Church to do? No lifting is too heavy for the Church to engage its mission and competently refute these accusations, these ideas that are contrary to biblical Christian interpretations. The Church has the answer for poverty. It ought to understand science better than anyone as it knows the Creator of all that is. The church ought to also be involved politically to uphold biblical ideals of marriage and family. It ought to also call out injustice, greed, and malice before anyone else. The Church ought not give up on society, but be proactive. However, it must know the *what* and the *why* of its beliefs and mission.

Unfortunately, because the word *apologia* means "a defense," many believe the use of apologetics is only about defending. That is only half of it. Apologetics must also be proactive with the truth. That's what we see in 2 Corinthians 10:3-5:

> *For though we walk in the flesh, we do not war according to the flesh, for the weapons of our warfare are not of the flesh, but divinely powerful for the destruction of fortresses. We are destroying speculations and every lofty thing raised up against the knowledge of God, and we are taking every thought captive to the obedience of Christ.*

Although Paul doesn't use the word *apologia* in this passage, it is clear he is writing about it. Describing his ministry, and perhaps even defending his actions, he wrote the above passage to the Corinthians. Clearly, Paul's reference to his ministry as warfare is proactive. When he wrote this, Paul was imitating Greek philosophers who often used this analogy in writing and speaking about the battle for ideas. He talks about how the weapons of our warfare are divinely powerful for the destruction of fortresses.

When Paul talks about fortresses and strongholds, some argue that he refers to spiritual powers, but a look at the context shows us differently. Paul was writing about ideas. He writes, "We are destroying speculations and every lofty thing raised against the knowledge of God." Clearly, Paul is going after speculations (*logismos*) or arguments, and every lofty thing that is raised against the knowledge of God. This is a proactive fight against wrong ideas.

From this passage we can intuit that before we can look at these arguments that are raised against the knowledge of God, we have to look at the God they are raised against. Too often our responses to attacks against Christianity are simple knee-jerk responses. As a result, our arguments either miss the point or sail passed the opponent's message. Knowing God is both a subjective and objective experience, I can know God through interaction with Him, and I can understand (know) what God is like. So many times God has shown mercy to me when I deserved something else. That is my personal experience of Him. However, I can also read about God and know Him through reasoning skills. I can learn something about God's attributes by reading the Bible and some of the classics like A. W. Tozer's *Knowledge of the Holy* and J. I. Packer's *Knowing God*. Too many times this kind of knowledge is overlooked.

Pursuing both systematic theology and biblical theology provides many rewards. We also must not overlook general revelation, which is knowing God through the natural order. This includes human reason as well as seeing God's handiwork in creation. The heavens declare the glory of God! Today we can not only look through telescopes and see God's glory, but we can also look through microscopes and see His wondrous ways.

Once we have begun pursuing the knowledge of God, we must then go on the offensive against the ideas that dispute who He is. Football and basketball use the term *offense* to describe periods of play when the team has the ball and tries to score points. However, it is in the military that this word finds its most compelling usage.

When an army attacks, it is on the offensive. Thus, it is not surprising that Paul uses the idea of an army several times to describe the Church. Here he uses the ideas of weapons, destruction, tearing down, and going on the offensive to describe the Christian lifestyle.

Remember, in Paul's world the Greek's used the language of war to describe the battle for ideas. The words *arguments* (NIV, NRSV, TEV) or *speculations* (NASB) are translated from a technical term for rhetorical or philosophical reasoning; the prisoners of war in this extended metaphor are human thoughts (cf. Proverbs 21:22).[13]

In this passage that focuses on the "destruction of fortresses" and "destroying speculations and every lofty thing raised against the knowledge of God," each verse reveals something about the task of apologetics. They reveal the offensive action of ministry: destroying fortresses, speculations, and every lofty thing raised up against the knowledge of God. Paul says they take the offensive and destroy fortresses.

Outside of Corinth stands a fortress on a mountain called the Acro-Corinth. It is a walled fortification once used in case of attack. The city residents would take refuge in this fortress and attempt to wait out the siege. Inside the fortress there would be water, food, weapons, and so forth. Generally, these fortresses (or strongholds) would be almost impossible to breach. So when Paul says they are destroying fortresses, this was the Corinthians' reference point. When they heard these words, they envisioned an army coming against a walled and impregnable stronghold and overcoming it.

When reading this passage we also need to put it in its context. Just prior to these verses, Paul was writing about his credentials and telling the Corinthians not to judge the apostolic team outwardly. He then launches into this discourse about the heart of his ministry. "Though we walk in the flesh, we do not war according to the flesh. Our weapons are not of the flesh but divinely powerful, powerful in God in order to destroy these fortresses" (2 Corinthians 10:3–4 author's paraphrase).

In light of this we must ask what kind of weapons Paul had, and whether we have the same weapons in twenty-first century America. The answer lies in whether or not we have the same enemy strongholds. Paul says his weapons are capable of destroying fortresses which he defines in the next sentence as speculations and every lofty thing raised against the knowledge of God. Although spiritual warfare can refer to direct assault by demonic powers, this doesn't appear to be what Paul is referencing. The word *speculations* is translated from the Greek *logismos.* In effect, Paul is referring to arguments or speculations raised against the knowledge of God. In Paul's day, he may have been referring to neo-Platonism, the beginnings of Gnosticism, Hedonism or other Greek philosophies.

Since the days of the early Church, people have always attempted to marginalize the Christian message by conflating it with other thoughts. As in the first century, our contemporary culture attempts to take the strength from Christianity by taking the miraculous from it, adding other themes, and imposing worldly thoughts on the eternal message. Thus, we can see that two things must be clarified before we engage in this warfare: our weapons and the strongholds we face. Our weapons are the same: first and foremost is the truth, and second is a sound mind to reason with. This is also known as critical thinking which can be defined as "thinking clearly and intelligently."

More precisely, *critical thinking* is the general term given to a wide range of cognitive skills and intellectual dispositions needed to effectively identify, analyze, and evaluate arguments and truth claims; to discover and overcome personal preconceptions and biases; to formulate and present convincing reasons in support of conclusions; and to make reasonable, intelligent decisions about what to believe and what to do.[14]

If we break this definition down, we first see it is to think clearly and intelligently. What a concept! This is the product of a sound mind that enables one to identify, analyze, and evaluate arguments, and truth claims. One thing the authors of the book *Critical Thinking: A Student's Introduction* state is that it is also possible to be objective in your thinking by overcoming personal preconceptions and biases. This is an important statement because one of the strongholds of today's society is that all thinking is perspective, and that we are all trapped in our own language because of biases. This indeed is a stronghold.

This definition finishes strong by saying that critical thinking is the ability to formulate and present convincing reasons in support of conclusions, and to make reasonable, intelligent decisions about what to believe and how to behave. This is critical thinking from a sound mind, one of the weapons of our warfare. Harnessed with truth, this is a powerful weapon.

We must also add to this our Christian character. How we live speaks as clearly as anything we can say. Few would see this as a weapon in the battle for ideas, but make no mistake. We are judged daily by how we live. Our credibility is a strong weapon in the battle for ideas. The media is quick to present ministers who fail in their personal lives. Several come to mind who were once prominent, but lost their place because they lacked character. This causes the world to look on the church and declare we are hypocrites. Although this is not fair as many Christians live good wholesome lives, it does give the world excuses to not consider the Church effective.

Today, there are at least four arguments that are raised against the knowledge of God. In order to address them, we must first have a clear understanding of the

God of the Bible, and the uniqueness of Jesus Christ. We can't come to understand the truth by looking at counterfeits, but we actually can recognize the counterfeits by knowing the truth.

An anecdotal story is often told of Queen Elizabeth II visiting Scotland Yard. (Whether this story is true or not doesn't affect the outcome). As the queen came to the counterfeiting department, she approached a man and said something to the effect of, "It must be difficult to remember all the counterfeits." The man replied, "No, your majesty, I only have to remember the real authentic one. All the others are then easy to spot."

This applies to our job as well. It doesn't do us any good to memorize what the cults or other religions believe if we don't know what good solid Christian doctrine is. Few people understand there are essential doctrines and non-essential doctrines. As Christians, we must learn to think biblically, theologically, and doctrinally.

As a culture, Americans are fairly biblically illiterate. Because of this, Americans are theologically unsound. Often New Age thought is considered more valuable than Christianity as is clearly seen by the number of Christians who read their horoscope, know their sign, and look at you strangely when you say you don't follow the stars. Americans tend to shy away from a particular view of Christianity, and accept a pluralistic view of many ways to God. It is easy to see that culture has had more of an effect on the Church than the other way around.

When it comes to recognizing the arguments and speculations raised against the knowledge of God, four come to mind readily—naturalism, relativism, pluralism, and the denial of the reliability of the New Testament. Almost every other argument whether philosophical, religious, cultic, scientific, or historical fits under one of these lofty thoughts.

61

Naturalism

Naturalism is the belief that the physical material world is all that exists. Denyse O'Leary explains the concept well:

> "**Methodological naturalism:** Scientists assume that all events have natural explanations.
>
> **Metaphysical** *(or Philosophical)* **naturalism:** Nature is all there is; there is no supernatural. The scientist assumes that religious beliefs cannot be true (my emphasis).
>
> **Scientism:** Truth can be discovered only through the scientific method. Anything that cannot be discovered in that way cannot be true. The scientist assumes that religious beliefs are a form of fraud."[15]

It is one thing to say that science cannot delve the realm of the soul because the soul is an immaterial substance. It is another thing to say that an immaterial substance does not exist because science cannot comment on it, experiment with it or observe it scientifically. So naturalism becomes the arbiter of what is real or not real.

Christians sometimes let atheists frame the argument, and say that faith and science or faith and reason are incompatible. Nothing could be farther from the truth. True science discovers knowledge and understanding through observation and experimentation. To sequester science to atheists, and make it sound like being a Christian would exempt someone from being a scientist is ludicrous. Many scientific disciplines were founded by Christians. For some, it wasn't their Christianity that drove them to science. Their Christianity was not the reason they chose to become scientists. We could say their Christianity was incidental. Others delved into science because they were Christians and were seeking to find God in the patterns of the universe.

It isn't science that is at odds with Christianity. It is naturalism that is at odds with Christianity—or to be more specific, metaphysical naturalism (what I called philosophical naturalism before). Metaphysical naturalism teaches that nature is all there is, and assumes the supernatural does not exist. In other words, it declares that only what science can affirm is real knowledge.

Of course, the problem with this idea is that the statement "only what science can affirm is real knowledge" cannot be affirmed by science or metaphysical naturalism! In fact, neither methodological naturalism (science assumes all events have natural causes) or methodological / philosophical naturalism can be affirmed by science. This is the principle of verifiability that A. J. Ayers proposed.

> "Such proponents as A. J. Ayer, following David Hume, originally claimed that for a statement to be meaningful it had to be either true by definition or else empirically verifiable through one or more of the senses. This proved too narrow, since on this ground the principle of empirical verifiability was not itself empirically verifiable. It too was meaningless."[16]

We should not confuse science for scientism or science with metaphysical or methodological naturalism. We should point it out when atheists or even agnostics do. Science is a valid discipline, and we have allowed it to be hijacked. Scientism is an ideology that affirms both types of naturalism, and asserts truth can only be discovered through the scientific method. It also asserts that any kind of religious belief is a fraud. This is not science.

Relativism (and Pluralism)

Relativism and pluralism are on the opposite end of the pole from naturalism. Where naturalism would look at evidence, in essence, relativism would ignore empirical evidence in favor of subjective feelings. Relativism rejects any absolutes. (Yes, it absolutely rejects absolutes.) Pluralism is the belief that no religion has all the truth. It asserts that every religion is valid. Pluralism is based on relativism, which asserts no absolutes exist anywhere, including religion. Relativism is expressed in two ways: epistemologically and morally.

Epistemology has to do with the idea of knowing; how we know what we know. Since relativism declares everything is relative, there is no truth except that which we decide to embrace. This means that truth is subjective; it has no absolute referent. So something can be true for you, but not for me. We have considered epistemological relativism in our view of truth. To say there are no absolute truths is an absolute truth, and therefore self-defeating. Relativism would say something can be "true for you, but not for me." Of course, a relativist would say that statement is true for everyone. In essence, the epistemological relativist says there is no absolute true or false.

Here's where critical thinking skills come into play. It is easy to be fooled by arguments that appear to be sophisticated or worse "feel good." Relativism feels good to so many, especially when it comes to religious ideas. We hear, "No one has the truth about God" or "There are many ways to God." These sound conciliatory, but they lack discernment, especially when we know the correspondence theory of truth because all religions make truth claims that contradict other religions.

For instance, Judaism contradicts Christian claims regarding Jesus being the Messiah. Islam denies the Trinity and Jesus as the Son of God. Buddhists are atheists, and Hindus worship thousands of gods. There's an often-quoted illustration of six blind men and an elephant that supporters of relativism like to quote.[17] (It sounds more like religious pluralism than relativism, but relativism is the mother of religious pluralism.)

The illustration of the Blind Men and the Elephant is based on an ancient Indian fable, and it goes something like this. The first blind man touches the elephant's side and claims it is a wall. The second man touches his tusk and claims it is a spear. The third man touches his trunk and claims it is a snake. The forth man touches his leg and claims it is a tree. The fifth man touches his ear and claims it is a fan. The sixth man touches its tail and claims it is a rope. In the last stanza of John Godfrey Saxe's poem about this fable, we find the point:

> So, oft in theologic wars
>
> The disputants, I ween,
>
> Rail on in utter ignorance
>
> Of what each other mean;
>
> And prate about an Elephant
>
> Not one of them has seen!

Notice that each man is blind and only the story teller knows it as an elephant. According to this, the pluralist is the only knowledgeable one concerning God. Everyone else is blind. Of course, Christianity is a revealed religion, and denies that the others are true.

However, the others also claim uniqueness, and deny the truth of other religions, too. The appeal of pluralism or religious relativism is that no one has a false view.

Moral relativism states that there are no absolute rights or wrongs. Where epistemological relativism claims there is no true or false, moral relativism claims there is no right or wrong, at least not an absolute right or wrong. However, society has to have rules because we can't live together without them. The question then is where do we get these rules?

There are two types of moral relativism or at least two ways it is explained. The first is that society decides what is right and wrong. What is best for the masses is one way to decide this. Laws are based on what will bring the most happiness or pleasure to the most people. Of course, this does not address the problem of injustice. If society decides that enslaving a particular part of the society is what brings the most pleasure to the most people, then slavery is instituted as law. Within this belief system, there is no real way to correct such an injustice. Of course, if we believe in moral relativism, we must say that it should not be corrected since society has deemed it to be correct moral behavior, and that any conflict with that moral behavior is rebellion.

This, of course, raises many questions about history's greatest injustices, like the Nazi death camps and apartheid. If those societies decided what was best for them, who are we to argue? Is there an unwritten code somewhere that says we can't take another people captive or exterminate a person if it pleases us? In the light of these questions, the logical progression of this belief is obvious.

It may seem ridiculous to us, but moral relativism has taken quite a hold in American culture. It is being played out in such issues as gay rights, same-sex or genderless marriage, abortion and bioethics, cloning and euthanasia. Our battle over these issues may seem hopeless, but when we see the philosophical foundation behind these arguments that are being raised against the knowledge of God, we are better equipped to defend the truth. If we can expose the contradictions of moral relativism, we will be better able to argue the Christian perspective.

The Reliability of the New Testament

This final argument is used to dismantle the Christian claim of Christ's resurrection. Many claim that the New Testament is unreliable because it has been copied so many times, and is filled with contradictions and mistakes. They argue that Paul was a woman-hating bigot who believed in slavery, and that Jesus was created by the imagination of His disciples. If He ever lived, He was just another man. The skeptics will say that there is no evidence of first hand accounts.

To counter this view, first we must understand that the gospels are records of the eyewitnesses of the resurrection. The questions we face are: *Are they credible witnesses? Is what they wrote then what we have now?* Remember, no one can prove to you that the Bible is the Word of God. It is a matter of faith to take the Bible as God's Word. This is not an argument for inspiration or inerrancy, just reliability. When dealing specifically with the New Testament, we have to discuss the eyewitnesses.

The eleven men who survived the night Jesus was betrayed were the most unlikely men to start a new religion. Just from a practical standpoint, these men were not nearly as sophisticated as some would suppose. After thousands of years of tradition, ritual and ceremony, eleven Galileans proposed a new religion that would challenge the status quo, and invoke the wrath of the Jewish priesthood and the Roman Empire. For what? All but one of these men died a violent death.

Is it reasonable to believe that, after hatching this plot to overthrow the Law of Moses and institute this new sect, they would die for this lie without gaining anything of substance? Wouldn't it be more reasonable to think that, after creating this ruse of Jesus rising from the dead, they would recant at first torture?

This was not the case. Rather they did die for this new faith, and they also did some other fairly unlikely things like including embarrassing reports of their own lack of faith. They wrote about "hard sayings," revealed themselves as missing the point at times, and admitted to running when Jesus was arrested. If in fact this was all an elaborate scheme, it would have been much more reasonable for them to fabricate a better picture of themselves.

Tradition tells us that the gospels were orally handed down. Oral tradition was common in the first century since most people were illiterate. Oral tradition is still common among people who do not have an alphabet or another way to pass on their history. At least three of the gospels were written before 70 AD, maybe all four. At that point, there was still plenty of time for contradictory evidence to be presented, but nothing has ever been found. The Jewish rabbis made record of Jesus, but of course it was in a negative light. Several non-Christian writers also recorded that the disciples believed Jesus had risen from the dead. In fact, several confirmed what the gospels said about Jesus (at least, they reported that the disciples believed this about Him). Considering that the early Church had no position of authority to fabricate and extend these stories, it really is quite a miracle that these confirmations exist.

Questionable Witnesses

Perhaps one of the most telling points of the eye-witnesses is the discovery of the empty tomb. In first century Palestine, women were not considered credible witnesses. Thus logically, if people were making up a story about a man being raised from the dead, they would find credible witnesses to help fabricate this lie. It is very doubtful that they would pick a woman of questionable reputation to be the first to make the discovery. Yet that is exactly what the New Testament records. Also, if we were creating this false religion would we project ourselves as cowards who ran and hid for fear of the Jews?

The Empty Tomb

Then there is the uncomfortable fact of the empty tomb. Some say the women were mistaken and went to the wrong tomb. However, Jesus' tomb had an address. It was the tomb of Joseph of Arimathea. Everyone could find that address. The problem with the empty tomb is that it remained empty because no one could give a reason for the body of Jesus being gone. The gospels tell us that the Jewish priests paid the guards to say the disciples had stolen the body while they slept. Of course, it seems unreasonable that the guards would know who had stolen the body while they were sleeping![18]

Luke tells us in the first chapter of his gospel that he wrote to Theophilus after researching and confirming from those who were eyewitnesses so that Theophilus would have the exact truth of what he had been taught. Thus, we can conclude that the eyewitnesses are reliable sources.

Now we ask, "Is what they wrote at that time still what we have now?"

When we look at ancient documents, we have to look at when they were written in relation to the events they were describing. The number of documents and consistency are vital pieces of information. With these considerations, as far as ancient documents go, it has been well established that the New Testament is the most historically accurate ancient document in existence. Most ancient documents, such as the writings of Julius Caesar, Homer and Plato, have a gap between the time they were written and the earliest copy of around 800 years. So if Plato wrote in 400 BC, the first copy we have would date somewhere around AD 400. In Plato's case, the gap is even wider.

For the New Testament, the gap is twenty-five to thirty-five years. We have a manuscript that dates around AD 115. If John wrote his gospel at the end of his life, after AD 80, that makes for a gap of around thirty-five years. It is possible that John wrote his gospel after AD 90. If this is correct, then we have only a twenty-five year gap! This is by all standards a very small gap in years from when a document was written to its earliest copy fragment.

We also have more copies of the New Testament than we do of any other ancient writing, and the number keeps rising. We have over 5,700 manuscripts in Greek. There are another 10,000 in Latin, with more in other languages. In all, we have nearly 25,000 documents. Besides this, there are the Church fathers who quote the New Testament almost in its entirety. From the second century through the thirteenth century there are a million quotes of the New Testament.

As far as internal consistency goes, not counting variance in spelling and word position changes, New Testament scholars have concluded that the documents are within 98 percent accurate—with *no* inconsistencies lending to a different theology. That is, despite any and all discrepancies, the New Testament says the same thing in all the copies and languages it has available. Therefore, we can safely say that what they wrote then is what we have now.

Central to the attack on the New Testament is the resurrection of Jesus. The resurrection is also the message of Christianity. If Jesus was not raised from the dead, we have no message. The resurrection of Christ must be defended. Several great scholars do a terrific job of defending the resurrection. Dr. William Lane Craig, Dr. Gary Habermas, Dr. Mike Licona, and Dr. Norman L. Geisler are among the best in defending the resurrection. I suggest studying any or all of these authors to become proficient in defending the resurrection.

Today, it doesn't take much insight to see that the Church lives in a hostile environment. Neither does it take much insight to see that we, the Church, need to understand the challenges we face, and the reality that God has equipped us to meet these challenges. If God is for us, who can be against us?

Chapter Five

ALWAYS BE READY

As an apologist, you can be well read, have a great vocabulary, and know which arguments apply to which philosophies. However, until you engage people, you will never know your state of readiness. Peter says, "...always being ready..." (1 Peter 3:15), describing a state of mind. We may be able to prepare for conversations in advance when we know the questions that will be asked. However, there will be times when people come up with an argument we don't know about.

A personal illustration will make this point clearer. Some of my earliest memories are of playing baseball. I grew up in Brooklyn, New York, when the Dodgers played there. Being a Dodger fan was not a choice but a birthright. My dad's blood was "Dodger blue," and so was mine. I have vivid memories of going to games. I knew nothing of basketball or hockey and very little of football, but I lived baseball. Like every other boy I knew, it was my dream to play big league ball.

My parents enrolled me in a newly founded little league when I was eight years old. It was 1956. I had been playing baseball in a true sandlot before then. I was around the age of six when my friends and I began self-organizing teams and playing rag-tag games in the sandlot. Of course, we did not have a new ball, and many times we used something without the outer "skin." Our bases were normally jackets or pieces of wood. We didn't have regulation bats, and our gloves were not very good. My glove was a small faux leather "toy" glove that was totally inadequate for catching a hard ball—and at that time there weren't many choices other than hardball.

Then, for my eighth birthday my dad bought me my first real baseball glove. We were living in a housing project in Brooklyn at the time. My dad was a cab driver and would always look for deals, and shop at some of the best places in New York City. For our birthdays, we got just one present; I had made my need for a glove to play ball clearly known. Thus, I waited with anticipation for my father to come through the door. My dad was not beyond practical jokes, and he walked in the house empty-handed. Neither my mother nor my sister knew he had rigged the box with the new glove in it so it was tied to his belt behind him. My disappointment was obvious when I saw him empty-handed. Then my dad turned around, revealing the glove. I was overwhelmed with excitement, hugging him tightly as he tried to take the package off his belt.

The glove brought me a level of equipment that was not normal for kids my age. As an eight year old, I was one of the smallest to try out for the league. This was not the sandlot any more. This was real baseball. The coaches put us through several drills, one of which I remember clearly. We were taught to put our hands on our knees, crouch, and "get ready." This basic skill was rehearsed over and over, time and time again.

Our ball field was in a public park, Marine Park, which had a dozen or so ball fields in the Mill Basin area of Brooklyn. Because it was public, it was not well maintained, which meant that small pebbles and rocks were strewn over the infield. For this reason, we had to always "be ready" for a *bad hop*. Simply put, a bad hop was what happened when the ball hit the ground where it could bounce in a variety of directions, depending on whether it encountered any rocks. There was only one action that could cut down on errors—to be ready. If the ball got by one of us, the coach would almost always yell out, "You weren't ready!"

This analogy from my little league days shows us the importance of being ready in the defense of our faith, too. When Peter wrote, "Always being prepared to make a defense to anyone who asks..." (1 Peter 3:15 ESV), he was writing in the context of persecution. These believers needed to be prepared to not buckle under the hand of the persecutor, but to give an account of the hope they had. Though persecution looks different for us, the same principle applies. In order to prepare for these situations, we must be ready.

As we've seen, to give an apology is to win someone who has an unfavorable view of us or what we believe to a favorable one. The simplest way to be ready is to learn the arguments and then rehearse the right response. When we do this, it is important to hear the arguments to learn why people who give these arguments believe what they do. If we don't do this, we will be tempted to give pat answers.

Always Getting Ready?

It's one thing to be ready and another to continually get ready before you do anything. The latter is an example not to follow. One lesson from history comes to mind. During the Civil War, General George B. McClellan was in charge of the Army of the Potomac. President Lincoln believed he had the best man for the job. McClellan was an excellent soldier who had ranked second in his class at West Point. His men loved him. He had an overwhelming force in the "battle of the peninsula," where he could have overtaken the Confederate capitol of Richmond. However, General McClellan continued to ask for more troops and more time to train. He continually overestimated the size of the enemy's force and underestimated his. He had a problem with readiness. He would never be ready, but was always getting ready.

We don't want to get into anything without being properly trained. However, we must reach a point when we consider ourselves ready. Knowing the basics is enough to engage people in the gospel conversation. No one knows all the answers, and it should not be a problem to say, "I don't know that, but I'll go and find out the answer for you."

A few things should come to light here. The first is the importance of being properly equipped. I had a glove that enabled me to play with the big boys. My dad had invested in a glove that would last me a few years. I also knew the basics of the game. Most of all, I learned how to be ready. I put my new equipment and skills to work. The combination of the equipment and the basic skills put me in the position to compete.

Too many Christians never get the right equipment and never learn the basic skills. Implementing apologetics is an art more than anything else. Although it is learning a set of skills, having the wisdom to know when to use them is also crucial. Without the knowledge of "being ready," it doesn't matter how much you know. McClellan was well-equipped and perhaps had the best knowledge, but he lacked one crucial piece. He never saw himself or his army as being ready.

Apologists prepare themselves by reading broadly about apologetics. Learning the general ideas of what apologetics are and why we practice them is crucial. Understanding the arguments against Christianity is also important. Knowing what scientific naturalism, relativism, and pluralism teach is also critical. These are the broad strokes. Having a general understanding of the history of ideas and why we think the way we do cannot be overestimated. There are so many opportunities to listen to audio recordings, watch videos, and read books and articles that there is no excuse to not be ready. Most who study apologetics know more about the evidence for Christianity than anyone they will argue with. Yet few get into the battle for ideas and engage people. They're always looking to learn something new so they can be "more" ready.

The amazing thing is I've learned a lot from the people I've spoken with. I've learned to understand their arguments and hear their hearts. It's not too difficult to learn who is a genuine seeker of truth and who just likes to argue. I never would have learned these things if I had waited until I thought I was ready enough.

Are you ready to defend your faith? Do you have a plan to get ready? If you are like me, you may have shrunk back from certain conversations because you were not prepared. However, being ready is something God requires of us: "Always be ready...." If God requires something of us, He also provides us with the answer or solution. In this case, He provides us with what we need to be ready.

Chapter Six

CONTEND

"We never seek a fight, but we dare not remain silent when the claims of Christ come under assault." (Chuck Swindoll)[19]

I was my high school's wrestling champ. In 1965 we didn't have inter-school competitions for wrestling, but I managed to beat everyone in my school in any weight class. Admittedly, I was fairly strong and quick. When I entered high school, we were taught the Greco-Roman style of wrestling (with a few modifications), and I picked it up quickly. It goes like this. Each of the opponents begins on the floor. One person kneels on all fours, and the other kneels beside him with one hand on the near forearm and other around the opponent's waist. Both combatants stayed in position until the gym teacher smacked the mat and yelled, "Go!" Then the struggle for dominance began.

The person on the top clearly had the advantage, but we learned moves to reverse the positions. The object was to pin the opponent or move him out of the ring. Points were scored for both. During the wrestling match, there is a lot of jockeying for position, rolling the opponent, struggling to get a power position, pushing with the legs, and trying to lock the other's arms. This was intense and difficult work, and there was no time-out—until one of the opponents was pinned or moved out of the circle. It was a constant wrestling that was sometimes exhausting.

This sort of wrestling was the context in which Jude wrote for the Church to contend, fight or wrestle for the faith that is foundational for the Church. "Beloved, while I was making every effort to write you about our common salvation, I felt the necessity to write to you appealing that you contend earnestly for the faith which was once for all handed down to the saints" (Jude 1:3).

This concept of wrestling fits nicely with this word *agonizomai* which means "to exert intense effort on behalf of something; contend." The short version of this word is "to struggle for." From it we get our word *agonize*. In other words, Jude is writing that we must wrestle, struggle, and agonize for the faith.

The Faith

The faith is also a term that must be taken in context. In this case, it is a belief system or a set of doctrines; it is not the dynamic faith that saves. This saving faith is explained in Hebrews 11:1, "Now faith is the assurance of things hoped for, the conviction of things not seen," and Ephesians 2:8, "For by grace you have been saved through faith; and that not of yourselves, it is the gift of God." By contrast, the faith mentioned here in Jude refers to the belief system of Christianity.

Jude writes about a system of belief, a doctrine or set of doctrines that was handed down once for all the saints. But others had come in and were corrupting the faith, so Jude reminded the believers to go back and remember the doctrine given to them by the apostles. This is not unlike Paul's admonition in Titus 1:9, "Holding fast the faithful word which is in accordance with the teaching, so that he will be able both to exhort in sound doctrine and to refute those who contradict."

Paul was exhorting Titus to hold fast the faithful word so that he would be able to both exhort in sound doctrine and refute those who contradicted the belief. This is a good example of contending for the faith.

Often Christians are unwilling to fight or they think it is wrong to argue for sound doctrine. Some may not even be aware of what sound doctrine is. We sometimes hear the cliché, "Doctrine divides." *Doctrine* is another word that has been hijacked. Some think we mean being dogmatic or having a dogma, which again has a negative connotation. But *doctrine* is a good word, and we should put it to good use. Doctrines can be essential to the truth of the gospel (such as the incarnation of Jesus) or nonessential (such as doctrines concerning the gifts of the Spirit). We must be able to discern essential from nonessential doctrine, and contend for that which is essential. I remember hearing someone say to me, "There are hills I would plant my flag on and die for, and there are others I would not." The essentials of the Christian faith are places I would fight for, plant my flag on, and stay there until someone else removed me.

Essentials

Dr. Norman Geisler and Dr. Ron Rhodes have an excellent book called *Conviction Without Compromise: Standing Strong in the Core Beliefs of the Christian Faith.*[20] This book outlines the essential doctrines of the evangelical faith. An essential doctrine is *not* one that people must believe in order to be saved. If that was the case, people would have to know an awful lot in order to receive salvation through Jesus Christ. No, an essential doctrine is one that must be true for the gospel to be true. In that sense, it is essential. Here's another way of explaining it: In order for the gospel to be true, these doctrines must also be true. So the gospel is dependent upon these doctrines for its truthfulness. If they don't exist or are not true, then the gospel is not true.

These essential doctrines include, but are not limited to the oneness of God, the divine Trinity, the Incarnation of Christ, Christ's impeccable (sinless) life, His vicarious death, His bodily resurrection, and so on. The authors list fourteen doctrines that are essential. That is, fourteen doctrines that must be true in order for the gospel to be true. To learn the rest of these doctrines, read their book, *Conviction Without Compromise.*

In this postmodern culture, it is more convenient and more acceptable to say we aren't dogmatic about holding to doctrine. Postmodernism is comfortable with contradictions because of its misuse and misunderstanding of tolerance. People who are influenced by postmodernism declare they are not "committed to" or "set" on a doctrine. The uninformed will give ground on the deity or humanity of Jesus. He or she will capitulate on the doctrine of hell and final judgment.

God is love, but love is not God. This is a misunderstanding. In the same way, God is light, but light is not God. These terms are not interchangeable. Misunderstanding the God of love—thinking that God and love are interchangeable terms—causes people to compromise related issues like same-sex marriage. Truly this is an emotional issue today, but it is also based on category mistakes like love is God and God is love.

Accepting the postmodern view of tolerance and political correctness can cause Christians to capitulate on essentials. Forgetting that God is also holy or suppressing the truth that God is holy will only give way to all sorts of non-biblical views. Contending for the faith means fighting for truth; not physically but ideologically.

Today, Christians are portrayed as intolerant bigots. That brings us to another term that has been hijacked—*tolerance.* It has come to mean something like this: "I must accept everyone's ideas or behavior as equally valid. If I don't, I'm intolerant which is a major mortal sin in today's society." What people really mean by *tolerance* is "suspending all judgment and critical thinking when we view someone else's beliefs or behavior." However, the irony is that those who support this idea of tolerance have already decided (judged) that this view of tolerance is good and my view is bad. In this way, they have judged me for judging and self-defeated their own position.

Tolerance does not mean I must accept someone else's beliefs as correct. It means I can disagree with the person's beliefs, but still respect that person. Jesus did not say we shouldn't judge, but that we should judge correctly and that we ought to be careful to judge righteously because we'll be judged by the same standard (see Matthew 7:2).

Suspending judgment or critical thinking is ideological suicide. I know I have had (and will most likely continue to have) stupid thoughts. It is crazy to suspend judgment on evil people—or on good people, for that matter. Today this idea has become so silly that we call people heroes who have never fought a battle, and we're afraid to let children lose at something because we think they'll be damaged psychologically—as if losing is not part of life. Here again we see that we have been losing the battle for ideas. This is the truth about tolerance: I can still love and respect the sinner while disagreeing with his or her behavior. I do not need to tolerate someone I agree with. It is the person I disagree with that I must tolerate.

Accommodating culture rather than contending for the faith seems to be the worst act of the Church. Culture puts pressure on the Church, makes us feel uncomfortable, and finally we capitulate to the new norms of ideas and behavior, stating that Christians can practice whatever they please as long as they keep it out of the public square. In the end, we find ourselves in a society that is distant from what we believe.

What?

Is there a direct connection between the fact that the Church has not contended for the essentials of the Christian faith and the condition of the world? It is not difficult to recognize that the world has continually become less respectful toward God and the Christian faith. We often hear of lawsuits to remove the Ten Commandments or Nativity scenes at Christmas time or crosses that were markers of someone's heroic acts. These are just some of the many legal battles fought over public Christian witness. The question is: Are the two related?

To be sure, when the Church does not stand up for what it believes, it loses influence. However, this is one step ahead of the problem. The Church has to first hold firm to these beliefs. As mentioned earlier, very few sermons expound the essential doctrines of the Scripture. Few catechisms are produced or practiced to teach doctrine to new believers and refresh older ones. Even if we are not comfortable with the word *catechism,* we ought to have courses that teach doctrine to new believers.

One prerequisite of this is that the Church must actually believe it has the truth. If we succumb to ideas of pluralism—that we are just one of several choices for religion—we grow indifferent to the plight of humankind, and the mission of God to bring honor to His name by declaring His excellence.

Romans 1:16-32 tells us that people are easily capable of suppressing the truth in unrighteousness. Do we, as the Church, contend with the world for the truth of God as Creator and Jesus as Redeemer? We easily condemn the world for its ungodly lifestyle, but have we contended for the truth of the gospel by finding common ground where we can wrestle in the arena for our ideas? Certainly, the Church's problems are the Church's problems. However, we are also the salt of the earth and the city set on a hill. This must mean something about the outcome of contending for the faith.

Of course, this admonition must be placed in the context of rhetoric. The Church must learn the art form of winning people to its position through skillful reasoning in the art of persuasion. This is also built on the idea of being ready. We must exemplify the meek and reverent spirit knowing that much of this problem has been created by our own lack of contending. This basically describes the *what* for which we must contend—the essential doctrines of the Christian faith. The question of *where* remains.

Where?

Where must we contend? In several of Ravi Zacharias' teachings, he describes the three places where ideas are formed, generated, and discussed. According to Ravi, ideas are formed at the university level, and they are generated at the media level. This level is also where they are dispersed throughout our culture. Then finally, these ideas are discussed around the dinner table, at the water cooler, on social media sites or wherever we have informal discussions.

I saw this confirmed in a part of the ancient world where many or most of our ideas about rhetoric were formed. On a visit to Athens, I received a clear picture of how this worked in ancient Greece. On top of the Acropolis stands the Temple of Athena which is called the Parthenon, as well as Nike's Temple, and several others. Not far from the top of the Acropolis stands the Aereopagus, Mars Hill, where Paul was taken in Acts 17. These two places were the universities of Paul's day. This was where views of religion and philosophy where discussed. On one side of the Acropolis stand two theatres which were the primary media points for ancient Greek culture. Just down the road is the marketplace. It still stands today. Without too much imagination, we can see how ideas were disseminated by the ancient Greeks. At the Acropolis and Mars Hill, the philosophers and poets worked out their philosophies, arguing between a few varieties of theism, polytheism, pantheism, and agnosticism.

The poets then wrote plays performed in the ancient theatres in which Epicureans and Stoics acted out their beliefs as entertainment for the public. From there, people began to discuss these ideas with others at the marketplace. Paul experienced this very thing in Acts 17 when he engaged the people on Mars Hill. It was here that they heard him declare the day of ignorance was over. Through this, we can clearly see the progression of ideas in our culture which also shows us where we need to go to have an influence.

How?

After the *what* and the *where* is the *how*. If the Church is to be influential in society, we need to have a presence in all three of the arenas of influence—the universities, the media, and the marketplace. Right now, we are barely in one. We preach our sermons to the choir every week, railing against the enemy's influence on society. But this has little impact on the world around us. If we want to become influential again, we must involve ourselves in every arena of culture.

First, we must get onto the university campuses and combat these ideas. Campus Christian groups exist, but at best, they are havens where Christians can retreat. Few seek to engage atheists. One organization that does do this is Ratio Christi.[21] *Ratio Christi* (RC) is Latin for

"The reason for Christ." Ratio Christi's goal is to win back the mind of the university for Christ. Working with other campus organizations, Ratio Christi sponsors debates, lectures, and evangelistic events. This is just the beginning of a movement, and they already have over one hundred chapters on college campuses. It is a good beginning, and I strongly encourage local churches to adopt a college to help start an RC chapter. However, first local churches must become those who contend for their faith.

Now let's talk about the media. On occasion we will see a celebrity Christian speak out for Christ on TV. We also see, on occasion, professional Christians represent a belief or give a review of a program or a discovery that may either question Christ's veracity or bring something to light. Professional journalists who are Christians rarely confess their orthodoxy, although we see it more today than before. Is this enough of a witness? Not at all. Here's what we need.

We ought to have Christian comedy writers as well as playwrights who write shows filled with biblically moral stories. Almost every TV sitcom is morally degrading and espouses the opposite of Christian values. Perhaps Christians complain about the state of morality on TV, but do nothing about it. Perhaps we undervalue or ignore the influence of TV (and other video media) when we ought to be more active. I know we wish it would go away. We wish we could come up with something to deny the influence it has on our children, but it is a fantasy to wish these things. Instead, we ought to be strategizing our influence to redeem what is there. We're investing our money to build great buildings, and we invest hundreds of millions to put on a good Sunday morning show. The problem is that the wrong people are showing up to watch, and we're not reaching the ones who need us most.

We have so many artists who profess Christ, but cannot express themselves without giving in to something worldly. This is a tragic loss for the Church. We keep saying the same thing, the same way, and wonder why no one understands or responds. Our young people respond to society's attempt at artistry far more than they do to what we have provided. Here's a need. We ought to address it and use it as a place to contend for our essentials by expressing the artistry God has given to us.

Finally, there is the marketplace where everyone works and lives. The major reason given for the average Christian's negligence in sharing his or her faith is fear—fear of not having an answer or not knowing how to express faith. How can we contend if we don't know who the enemy truly is or what the rules, weapons, and nature of the fight are? Sadly, not many local churches or ministries teach apologetics? Not many teach critical thinking skills. Far too few are involved in it, and far too few leave it up to the individual to learn anything about apologetics. This must change.

Dr. Al Mohler, president of Southern Baptist Theological Seminary, has said that every ministry of the twenty-first century must be an apologetic ministry.[22] In this way, the Church will be equipped for this important work of contending for the faith. Every church needs to have at least one resident apologist, and most of all, pastors must preach apologetics sermons regularly.

Clearly, as we have seen, contending for the faith is crucial for the Church. This is why we need *Apologetics for the Rest of Us*—for the common person, not just the scholar. If we lose these essentials of the faith, we lose our compass. We also lose our witness to the uniqueness of the gospel. We must not passively let this happen. Instead, we must contend.

Combine this idea of contending with the previous chapter about being ready. Are you ready to contend? Are you in position to take on an argument? Do you believe the gospel is worth contending for? I believe it takes the right attitude to engage in apologetics, and God is providing the necessary equipment in order to be in the battle.

Chapter Seven

COMMON GROUND

Finding common ground—a place that enables us to speak to others—is an important part of apologetic work. Actually, it is important in any preaching situation. Acts 17 provides us with a great example in the ministry of the apostle Paul. As Paul preached to both Jews and Gentiles, he adapted his message to each audience. He used both rhetoric and common ground to win his listeners' ears. Here is a more than useful example of winning hearts and minds.

> *Now when they had traveled through Amphipolis and Apollonia, they came to Thessalonica, where there was a synagogue of the Jews. And according to Paul's custom, he went to them, and for three Sabbaths reasoned with them from the Scriptures, explaining and giving evidence that the Christ had to suffer and rise again from the dead, and saying, "This Jesus whom I am proclaiming to you is the Christ." And some of them were persuaded and joined Paul and Silas, along with a large number of the God-fearing Greeks and a number of the leading women.* (Acts 17:1-4)

Acts 17 is a rich example of apologetics. Let's go over some ideas we've already discussed. Remembering that Luke was a Greek who became a Christian enlightens the reader even more. Luke explains that when Paul arrived in Thessalonica, he went to the synagogue for three Sabbaths, and *reasoned* with them from the Scriptures, "explaining and giving evidence." Luke is demonstrating Paul's method in rhetorical terms. Here Luke shows how Paul used this art form to reach the Jews. Then, he cements the concept by saying, "Some of them were persuaded and joined Paul and Silas as well as a large number of God-fearing Greeks and a number of leading women."

Interestingly, Luke uses terminology that shows Paul's use of the art of rhetoric as he preached to the Jews. Unlike Peter in Acts 2, who preached his sermon to the Jews gathered in Jerusalem, Paul uses rhetoric—that is, he moves them persuasively from a position that was basically ignorance to a favorable position. This allowed the Holy Spirit to move on their hearts. The use of apologetics has been described as removing the mental obstacles that preclude people from seeing the gospel. Here through rhetoric Paul reasons, explains, and provides evidence that Jesus had to suffer and die in order to redeem people from their sins.

It is no accident that Luke, who was a Greek, uses this language to describe Paul's ministry. When we understand rhetoric, we can see why Luke demonstrates Paul's ministry this way. This was very much a part of first century Greek thinking, and Luke, as a Greek, understands this. We also have to remember that Paul was not raised in Jerusalem (though he had training there), but in Tarsus which is located in present Turkey. He understood the Hellenistic Jew. In other words, he understood Greek culture intimately, and when speaking to Hellenists he employed rhetorical principles.

Many accept this method Paul used as an example even though they don't know or understand Luke's emphasis on rhetoric. Many also extol Paul's visit to Thessalonica as an example because of the outcome. However, Acts 17 has a special place in apologetics. Look at Paul's visit to Athens:

> *Now while Paul was waiting for them at Athens, his spirit was being provoked within him as he was observing the city full of idols. So he was reasoning in the synagogue with the Jews and the God-fearing Gentiles, and in the market place every day with those who happened to be present.* (Acts 17:16-17)

Athens

Many think Paul's visit and ministry to Athens was a failure based on the outcome. However, I think we must keep the context of Paul's ministry to Thessalonica in mind. Clearly when Paul was in Thessalonica, he ministered to Jews in the synagogue, and therefore could use Scripture. However, in Athens he ministered not only to Jews but also to non-Jews, pagans in the marketplace, and then on Mars Hill.

Paul's trip to Athens reveals his sensitivity and ability to address diverse audiences. Although he spoke in the synagogue in Athens, he also spoke in the marketplace where people gathered each day to speak of "something new." Athens was known as the seat of learning for the Greeks. This is where Socrates, Plato, and Aristotle taught their philosophies, as well as many other Greek poets and philosophers. Athens was the center of Greek learning, and it influenced the entire Roman Empire. Although the Greeks were not dominant as a military empire since they had been conquered by the Romans, their philosophy was imbibed in Roman life. Greek culture permeated the Roman Empire, and Greek thought was central to many. The effect of Athens and Greek thought far outlived the Greek Empire. The culture, architecture, philosophy, and knowledge continued on among the Romans, and as a result Athens continued to be *the* seat of learning.

As people approached Athens by sea, they could see the Acropolis dominating the landscape. It is said that a statue of Athena stood in the Parthenon. Athena held a spear with a golden blade which stood above the height of the Parthenon (there was no roof), and the spearhead could be seen glimmering in the sun from miles out at sea. Even in ruins, the Acropolis is impressive with its stately columns, various temples, and magnificent statues. The friezes (carvings) on the Parthenon are still examples of the Greek commitment to beauty and detail. It is in this city that we find Paul interacting with Stoic and Epicurean philosophers. His message brought "strange things" to their ears, so they brought him to Mars Hill, the Areopagus (see Acts 17:18–20).

Mars Hill

Mars Hill is not an attractive or recognizable place, but is located just below the Acropolis. It is renowned as the place where philosophers gathered, but also a place of judgment. The ancient path to the top of the Acropolis remains to this day. There is also a set of stone stairs you can take to the top of Mars Hill. There is a small section of rocks that would make for seats and an open space where a speaker could stand. Visiting Mars Hill was my personal highlight on my first trip to Athens. There's nothing particularly memorable about Mars Hill—no statues or no temples, just rock. But this is where Paul addressed the philosophers of his day.

Because Mars Hill is overshadowed by the Acropolis, when you're standing on top you can't help but notice this glorious tribute to the history of the Greeks. As a student of Scripture and apologetics, it is more than rewarding to rehearse Acts 17. Paul's words echo in your ears:

> *Men of Athens, I observe that you are very religious in all respects. For while I was passing through and examining the objects of your worship, I also found an altar with this inscription, "To an Unknown God." Therefore what you worship in ignorance, this I proclaim to you.* (Acts 17:22-23)

Paul's brilliance is seen here as he addresses this august group of men. He begins as a visitor would by complimenting his audience (this is a rhetorical principle). Then he pays respect to them by telling them he has examined their objects of worship and recognized an altar to this "unknown" deity.[23] Whether Paul knew the story behind this unknown God or not is immaterial. He knew enough to use it as common ground to tell the Athenians about Jesus. Telling them the day of ignorance is over, he launches into a theistic description of God:

> *The God who made the world and all things in it, since He is Lord of heaven and earth, does not dwell in temples made with hands; nor is He served by human hands, as though He needed anything, since He Himself gives to all people life and breath and all things.* (Acts 17:24-25)

In what translates as one extended sentence, Paul declares God as maker of the world and all things in it. "Therefore," Paul concludes, "God cannot dwell in handmade temples or be served by human hands as if

He would need anything because He in fact gives life and breath to all things." Paul presents the cosmological and a piece of the teleological message to the Greeks (we'll discuss these two arguments later), who had various views of the universe and how it came to exist. As he goes on, he reveals God's providence and sovereignty:

> *And He made from one man every nation of mankind to live on all the face of the earth, having determined their appointed times and the boundaries of their habitation, that they would seek God, if perhaps they might grope for Him and find Him, though He is not far from each one of us.* (Acts 17:26-27)

Though Paul does not mention humanity's separation from God, he alludes to the need for God in verse twenty-seven. Can you see Paul's mastery of Greek thought and how he relates it to the truth of God? These verses connect directly to Romans 1:16-32. Thus, Paul uses what is easily recognizable to the Greeks to reveal the God of Heaven. He reminds them that God has "determined their appointed times and their boundaries," and he goes so far as to quote Epimenides, one of their poets:

> *For in Him we live and move and exist, as even some of your own poets have said, "For we also are His children."* (Acts 17:28)

Paul announces that if we are children (offspring) of God, we should not think God is correctly represented by gold or silver or that He can be formed into an image by the hands of humans. The Greeks were divided over these ideas. Stoics and Epicureans debated the idea of God all the time. Paul knew this, and he used their ideas as a basis for presenting the biblical God.

Common Ground

> *Therefore having overlooked the times of ignorance, God is now declaring to men that all people everywhere should repent, because He has fixed a day in which He will judge the world in righteousness through a Man whom He has appointed, having furnished proof to all men by raising Him from the dead.* (Acts 17:30-31)

At this point, some of the philosophers sneered at him though others said, "We shall hear you again concerning this" (Acts 17:32). The chapter goes on to say that a few people began to follow Paul afterward. This is an incredible passage. Paul's address on Mars Hill was not, as some think, a failure. I respectively disagree with this position. Although we don't see a mass conversion, we do see some chose to follow the Lord. However, my point is not in the number of people who responded, but in the method Paul used to address them. Paul used his rhetoric and apologetic skills to present the gospel. He stood on common ground by accepting who they were as religious people, and then used their worship of an unknown God to announce that the day of ignorance was over.

Paul reasoned with them, explaining and giving evidence much in the same way as he did with the Jews in the beginning of Acts 17. What we can identify clearly is that Paul adapted to his audience. He adjusted *how* he declared Jesus as the Christ. To the Jews in the synagogue in Thessalonica, Paul could use the Scriptures as evidence and explain to them about the Messiah. The Jews would be looking for the Messiah, and would have much debate as to what the Messiah would do and how and what He would accomplish. Few, if any, Jews thought the Messiah would have to suffer and die. Paul made it clear to them that the Scriptures revealed that.

One criticism of Paul's trip to Athens is that he didn't use Scripture and, therefore, had few results. Again, I humbly disagree with this. What Paul did in Athens was to find common ground with these Athenian scholars in order to launch into a description with which they could relate. Not many people can go to the top thinkers of a different belief system, preach to them, and reach some of them with the message of the gospel. It is unfair to compare this with Acts 2, where Peter preaches his sermon on the day of Pentecost. Peter preached to Jews who had been talking about this man Jesus. There were rumors that Jesus had risen from the dead—not to mention the supernatural visitation of the Holy Spirit. As I said, it is an unfair comparison.

In Thessalonica, the Scripture was the common ground Paul used to reason, explain, and give evidence about the atonement to the Jews. In both cases Paul employed an apologetic argument based on rhetorical skills. He found common ground, reasoned, explained, and gave evidence that Jesus was alive from the dead.

In Athens Paul used what the Greeks knew about and could relate to. He reasoned with them about the person of God, and illustrated these ideas with concepts they could relate to by using reason and logic. He then proclaimed that God had appointed this man, Jesus, to judge the living and the dead. In the end some sneered, but some were persuaded. This is the correct pattern for speaking to unbelievers and skeptics.

If we lined up Luke's description of what Paul did in Thessalonica and what he did in Athens, we would see that in both instances he used common ground, explained, gave evidence, and finally proclaimed the risen Jesus. He did this with both the Jews and the Gentiles. If they knew Scripture, Paul could use it. When they had no Scripture, he still found common ground by adapting to his audience without compromising his message. Paul's address to the gathering on the Aerepagus is a brilliant piece of apologetic preaching.

This is exactly how apologetics and rhetoric ought to work. Luke gives us a template for how to present Christ as Lord and Savior. In both cases we see Paul adjusting to his audience, but in essence preaching the same message. Apologists must learn to do this if we are going to reach a culture that is far from us.[24]

It ought to likewise be obvious that Paul also adjusted to his audience. I say this in order to state the obvious. When Paul went to Thessalonica, he was in the synagogue with the Jews. After going to Berea, Paul goes to Athens, and there we see him adjusting once again to reach his audience. He adjusted and found common ground. Someone who truly wants to reach people with the power of the Gospel will seek to find common ground, and thereby gain a place of influence with that audience.

Chapter Eight

CERTAINTY—POST EVANGELISM

Certainty is one of those things that everyone really wants. I want to know that the plane is going to leave at the scheduled time of departure. I want to be certain that my car will make it to the end of the trip I'm taking. These examples are not the same as mathematical certainty, like two plus two will always equal four or the square root of nine is three. Mathematical certainty is one kind of certainty. Another kind of certainty is certainty beyond a reasonable doubt. Most of us live with this kind of certainty every day, whether we are aware of it or not.

However, in the second kind of certainty, we can be certainly wrong. To insure we won't be wrong, we do a better job of researching what could go wrong. I have my car serviced and looked over by a trustworthy mechanic to make sure or make certain it can make the trip. I may check the departure time on this flight to see how many times it leaves late. In the end, I must still step out on what I know. The more I know about something, the more "sure" I am and the more certain I become. This is the case Luke makes in writing to Theophilus in both his gospel and the Book of Acts.

*Inasmuch as many have undertaken to com-
pile an account of the things accomplished
among us, just as they were handed down
to us by those who from the beginning were
eyewitnesses and servants of the word, it
seemed fitting for me as well, having inves-
tigated everything carefully from the beginning, to write it out for you in consecutive
order, most excellent Theophilus; so that you
may know the exact truth about the things
you have been taught.* (Luke 1:1-4)

To this end, Doug Powell's *Holman Quick Source
Guide to Christian Apologetics* (a must for your research)
tells us that when we are trained in apologetics we
acquire boldness, security, and a lack of defensiveness.
Apologetics enable the believer to engage the world
without acquiescing to it and without compromise. [25]

In other words, we become more certain of what
we believe. This is essential for our Christian witness.
Some people believe that training in apologetics will
affect our faith negatively, but they are wrong. It will
affect our faith, of course. It will make it stronger. Luke
wrote to Theophilus that he researched by investigating
everything from the beginning, "...so that you may know
the exact truth about the things you have been taught"
(Luke 1:4). The English Standard Version translates
this verse, "...that you may have certainty concerning
the things you have been taught."

Luke was meticulous in his research and provided
exact truth concerning things that we might consider
small. However, Luke got political figures, dates,
customs, and many other details right. In his second
writing, the Book of the Acts of the Apostles, we find over
eighty verifiable facts concerning geography, people,
dates, offices, and government officials. Luke got it right
all the way. Apart from Luke's disposition to provide

meticulous coverage of the life of Jesus and the work of the apostles is the outcome of his labor, "that you would have certainty...."

When Christians study the reasons for their faith, turn over all the rocks, and dig into all the corners to find evidence, they only become more certain of their faith. When we become more certain, we become bolder, more confident, and more secure in sharing our faith. The number one reason that Christians give for not sharing their faith is fear. Fear is a powerful motivator that causes us to hide our light under a bushel. However, when we know the truth of Christianity is backed up by evidence—that we have the most historically reliable ancient documents, that there is scientific evidence for God's existence, that the resurrection of Jesus is not only testified to in the gospels and epistles, but through non-Christian writers—we then have certainty. We then become bold, secure, and non-defensive, and can correctly argue for our faith.

The Real Jesus

As we learn to defend our faith confidently, there's one important detail we must consider—who the *real* Jesus is. We live in an anti-intellectual society, and unfortunately, the Church has fallen right in with the crowd. Somehow, we have bought into the idea that using our minds is counter-productive to our faith. This could not be farther from the truth.

Consider this: Our faith is only as strong as the object we place it in. Some may say, "My faith is in Jesus." That sounds good, but the question is which Jesus? Is it the Jesus of the New Testament? The Mormon Jesus? What about the Jehovah Witness Jesus, the New Age Jesus or the Buddhist Jesus? As Christians, we might be tempted to say, "The real Jesus." But we have to ask ourselves why our view of Jesus is better than these others. What evidence do we have that our Jesus is the right one and that, for example, the Mormons are not right? A bit of study may be in order to ascertain just which Jesus is the real Jesus.

Luke wrote about certainty, and that is exactly what is missing among our young people. They have been told to just believe (blind faith) with no evidence for what they believe. Then they get assaulted at the university with questions about whether the New Testament is credible or how anyone could deny the evidence of natural selection. They're confronted with arguments that Jesus is a mythical figure, and that believing in someone being raised from the dead is like believing in the tooth fairy or Santa Claus.

For this reason, statistics for the number of young people who leave the Church in their late teen years range from 50 percent to 85 percent. Ten percent would be too much—and unfortunately, we are looking at a much larger number than that. We should not lose *any* of our young people to arguments presented against a biblical worldview because there is so much evidence for it. In the least, we ought to equip the Church with the evidence we have.[26]

Older Christians just don't seem to be bothered. They're not concerned about the evidence because they believe what they believe. There seems to be a lack of any sense of urgency. It appears that not much will get under their skin to move them to action. However, this is an inadequate response to give to those who are struggling with what they believe. What we don't realize is that our faith is eroded when arguments go unanswered or we become complacent in our faith.

This is what Paul was talking about when he told the Corinthians that he was "taking every thought captive to the obedience of Christ" (2 Corinthians 10:5). Either we take thoughts captive or they will take us captive. Those who sit under secular professors who untiringly present natural selection as the engine that runs all biological life soon become persuaded to consider the possibility. Eventually, they usually compromise their faith to subscribe to secular views *unless* they have evidence to the contrary.

Nearly every spring, when the Church celebrates the resurrection of Jesus, some new "evidence" is discovered to discredit the New Testament claims. Jesus' wife will be presented, His tomb will be found or another epistle will be uncovered with damaging reports of the gospels. Of course, none of this is ever contested by biblical authorities who could speak intelligently about the so-called evidence. So many people never seem to understand that television is all about ratings—not about facts or truth. Nevertheless, apologists (myself included) often get calls and emails asking whether we have seen the special about the Gospel of Judas—or some other fable. Sometimes the dramatic productions appear convincing, and those who don't know the difference can be taken captive by these presentations. Once again, this is why we need apologetics.

Training in apologetics and critical thinking skills will help individuals dispense with the nonsensical distortions of New Testament truth. Learning the evidence for a biblical worldview only serves to strengthen the believer and equip the Church.

Will there ever be a time when doubts will not enter your mind? No! The kind of certainty we're looking at in this chapter is not mathematical certainty. You know two plus two will always equal four. This kind of certainty is beyond doubt. But here I am talking about the kind of certainty you have when you get in your car to go on a trip. The more research you do on the evidence for Christianity, the more certain you will be of its truthfulness. Your faith will grow according to that which you are certain of. Luke wrote to Theophilus that he would know the exact truth of what he had been taught. Compile the evidence for Christianity and your faith will become more certain.

PART THREE

Chapter Nine

APOLOGETICS AND WORLDVIEW

I remember hiking up a path and turning to look out over the valley I had just left. Quite a view! However, the higher I climbed the path, the more the view changed; I had a different perspective of the valley. Later I boarded a plane, and as we flew over that area, I recognized the valley below. Wow! I saw another perspective of the same valley.

From the first vantage point, I could look out at the valley and make sense of its contours, cliffs, and other distinctive features. However, from the second vantage point I saw things differently. Finally, from the aircraft I had a completely different view and again changed what I thought about this valley. Worldview is very much about how you see the world—but also about what influences how you see. Worldview is about viewing the data around you, and then interpreting it in order to make sense of reality.

Another illustration that serves well comes from a good friend of mine. Chris is a brilliant man. I often joke with him that he is a storehouse for "odd facts and uninteresting information." However, after a few minutes with Chris, you know you are talking with someone at a genius level.

Until recently, many people didn't know Chris had a learning disability and always struggled with learning, especially reading. Later in Chris' life, he discovered he had a type of dyslexia that made words on a page look very strange. Not only were letters out of place, but they appeared raised on the page. After some serious testing, the technician testing Chris began to put lenses of different colors in front of the printed page. When one particular color was over the text—*Eureka!*—the words appeared "normal" and flattened to the page. Chris could read like the rest of us. Chris now wears these colored glasses to see the world.

This illustration serves to demonstrate how a biblical worldview works. When you get the biblical worldview right, everything appears normal.

In this chapter, I want to discuss my worldview about worldviews. I've lost count of the books I've read on worldview. I burned through them like a hungry man at a hamburger stand. The most frustrating issue about worldview is a simple definition. If you read the books I've read, you will come up with several sentences of description for several different perspectives. Some include the same things and others don't. None give a concise definition.

I first encountered this confusion about worldview as I delved into the world of apologetics. In my study of apologetics, I became aware that many books and speakers spend a lot of time describing *how* to do apologetics. Some also discuss *why* we ought to do apologetics, and these are definitely proper studies. However, several writers use the term *worldview* quite a bit, which caused me to begin asking questions about the term. *Do we all mean the same thing when we're talking about worldview?* I thought I knew what a worldview was, but I had never really studied it. I wanted some definitive answers. That was much easier said than done.

When I study a subject like this and don't find a definitive answer to my question or questions, I tend to summarize and boil things down. One of the frustrating things about studying worldview is that no one has all the answers. Some writers like James Sire say you must ask six questions concerning reality or what is "really real." Other authors list up to twelve questions—each one attempting to get answers about reality. All of the questions stemmed from metaphysics, and as I began to analyze the questions, I saw that they fell into a few categories, four to be exact.[27] With this understanding, instead of being tied to specific questions, we can acknowledge the categories and begin to ask questions about them. These are the four categories we must ask questions about.

Truth

The first category is truth or knowledge. If we cannot agree on this category, there is no sense in following through on the other categories. Truth—or how we know the truth—is always the first place to start.[28] If we think truth is relative, unknowable or nonexistent, we have come to some understanding. In a conversation, this is where we can show a person that to deny the truth is a self-defeating exercise, as we covered in an earlier chapter. Make no mistake; if we miss this step, we will have to return to it again.

God

Once we establish truth, we can move on to category two: God or ultimate reality. The first big question is this: Is there a God? If people do not believe in God, the discussion moves to the next category. If they believe there is a God, they can move on to a second level with questions like these: What kind of God is he/she/it? Is

God personal or impersonal? Is there more than one god (polytheism)? Is God finite or infinite (finite godism)? Is God everything (pantheism)? Does God participate in His creation (theism/deism)?

Humanity

The third category relates to our understanding of humanity. What is humanity? Are we animals? Are we the product of a blind evolutionary force like natural selection or the product/creation of a specific act of God(s)? The answer to this question leads us to ask: Is humanity moral? Is there a way people ought to live? Do people have a destiny or purpose?

The Universe/Nature

When we ask questions about the other categories, we ultimately come to this category. Just what is the universe? Is matter all that exists? Is the universe God (pantheism)? Is it growing? And so forth.

The questions I listed in each of these categories are not exhaustive, but they will help us understand our own worldview and that of others. We cannot underestimate the role a worldview plays. So here is my take on worldview, as garnered from several books.

A Definition

A *worldview* is the way we look at the world and take in the information we receive. We do this in order to make sense of the world, to structure our beliefs, and make decisions. In turn, worldviews affect our thinking as a grid where we place objects of knowledge we acquire.

Both individuals and societies have worldviews. An illustration that serves both the individual and society helps to explain how worldviews work. When we look at a corporate worldview, we have to look at culture, too. Culture is the outward expression, the soul of a society. Here's an illustration that has helped me.

Consider a tree. Pick your favorite. When you look at the tree, what do you see? First you see the leaves, maybe the branches, and possibly the trunk of the tree. However, what you're looking at is what is above the ground. Now think about the system that feeds the tree. Although some nourishment comes through the leaves, the tree is primarily fed by the root system.

Applying this analogy to worldview, what the leaves, branches, and trunk are to the tree is what culture is to society. What the roots are to the tree is what worldview is to society. The culture of society is its soul; this is what we see and come into contact with. Culture is made up of things like education, the arts, science, politics, entertainment, government, and many others. By contrast, the roots are what feed the tree, keep it healthy or cause it to be sick. These are not easily seen, but they are very important. The roots of society are its beliefs about truth, God, humankind, and the universe. In order to change a society and affect its culture, we must change its root system.

When people say, "America has changed," they generally think the culture has changed. However, the real change has happened in the roots of society. People's view of truth has changed from an absolute view of truth to a relative view of truth—or even a flat out denial of it. The view of God has changed from a biblical view of God to a pluralistic view of deity. Thus, the culture war is really a worldview war because it is worldviews that are in conflict.

When it comes to a personal worldview, we can see that a societal worldview is made up of the people who are allowed to participate and contribute to it. In America, the personal worldviews that affect the societal worldview are those of professors at universities, the media, and politicians. Generally, they're the ones who participate in and contribute to the corporate societal worldview. They shape the way individuals think about truth, God, humankind, and the universe.

When we understand the importance of worldview, it will change the way we talk with people. When we are interacting with or engaging people in conversation and believe we have an opportunity to share the gospel, we can begin to question people's views on the four categories. We must find out what their worldviews are beginning with truth. If we can't ascertain how to judge any statement as true or false, we may end up in a meaningless conversation.

In *Making Sense of Your World: A Biblical Worldview,* the authors (Philips, Brown, and Stonestreet) explain four tests to test the validity of a worldview. One is the test of logic which asks these questions: Is it reasonable? What is the evidence? Does it fit reality? Does it satisfy? Worldviews give explanations for what is real, and they should give us logical reasons for whatever we believe. A biblical worldview is logical, has evidence, fits reality, and satisfies the intellect as well as the emotional side of life.

To say that everyone has a worldview is to say nothing more than everyone has a way they navigate life. Few people actually try to make sense out of life. Most people don't know how they navigate, and they simply live with an inherited worldview. Few people actually think about the categories suggested here in order to logically determine how to live. Most live on autopilot, bouncing off things like a billiard ball. Few investigate the categories and make decisions on how life ought to be lived and—even better—how to relate to others with differing worldviews.

Only when life begins to collapse or they encounter a situation that causes them to pause do some people begin asking questions. Sometimes it is a crisis of life, the loss of a loved one, the loss of a job, having a baby or becoming an empty nester. Sometimes people have to consciously look at one or more of the categories in order to get some bearings and take the next step. This is when they encounter their worldview. These are opportune times to help people discover the biblical worldview and present to them the living Lord Jesus.

Unfortunately, many Christians also live on autopilot and haven't thought very deeply about their faith. They may even look differently at their social and private lives. Socially, they may live in the way of the world, but privately they may confess Christianity. This is not a coherent worldview, but is a compromise and misunderstanding of the nature of a biblical worldview. It is misunderstanding what it means to be a Christian.

This is a big part of the problem. Many Christians have not thought deeply, if at all, about their faith. In order to become a culture-influencing force, we must first become aware of our own worldview, and then learn how to lead others in worldview discovery.

Discovering our worldview and its veracity is extremely important. The first step is to recognize that we have a worldview. However this is just the beginning. Understanding what we are supposed to defend is crucial to our task. It ought to be obvious that the more informed we are the stronger our faith will become, as our faith is only as strong as the object we place it in. To make sense of reality, we have to properly view reality, and then interpret it. Worldview is the way we do this, and the biblical worldview is the correct way to view reality.

Chapter Ten

ARGUMENTS FOR GOD'S EXISTENCE

Now that we've discussed worldview, let's consider what it is that we believe. Obviously, I do not have room in this book to thoroughly cover this subject. This is intended as a beginner's guide, so my arguments for a biblical worldview are not very sophisticated. We will stick to the basics. However, I will present enough here to get you started in understanding the evidence for God's existence, His design, and the moral law. Some of the language and reasoning I use in this chapter may sound more complex than the rest of this book. This is where most books on apologetics start. I, at least, have given you a primer leading up to these arguments. As I said before, the study of apologetics is heavy lifting. There's no way around it.

Many times these arguments are cumulative. Therefore, we make a cumulative case from them. At times, just one of these arguments is enough to persuade people to change their position about Christianity. However, when these arguments work together, they make a strong case. In essence what we are attempting to do is make a reasonable argument for our case.

For Christianity to be reasonable, it must give cogent, compelling arguments about reality. It must be able to present answers for questions like: Why is there something rather than nothing? Although, this is one of the most basic questions, few people can adequately answer it. "Because God willed it," is an inadequate answer or at least an incomplete answer. In other words, it is a pat answer. The appropriate response to this pat answer is, "Which God?"

The Cosmological Argument

The cosmological argument(s) are about the beginning of the universe. Dr. Norman Geisler writes:

The basic idea of this argument is that, since there is a universe rather than none at all, it must have been caused by something beyond itself.[29]

Everything that has a beginning has a cause. The universe has a beginning. Therefore, the universe has a cause. This is the simple logic of the argument. If the universe had a beginning, then the universe has a cause. Was the cause an accident or was the cause purposeful? If the cause was accidental rather than purposeful, we have no need to proceed with the explanation.

Now the question is: Can something come from nothing? Nothing in this sense is a philosophical term that in this case means "non-being"—it has no existence. Can something that doesn't exist cause something else to exist? I think the reasonable answer is, "No."

Thus, something must have caused the universe to exist. Is the *something* a person or a force? That has to be decided by more evidence, but for now we can say that "nothing" cannot produce something. Therefore something produced the universe.

It was Einstein who taught us that time, space, and matter are related in the sense that we cannot have one without the others. Once we have matter and space, we have time. Time doesn't exist on its own since it is a measurement of movement. We measure time by the rotation of the earth and the circumnavigation of the earth around the sun. This is an object moving through space in a certain amount of time. What we are saying is that there was an instant when all of this came to be. Thus, whatever caused matter, space, and time to come into existence is outside all three of them.

We know the universe is not eternal and that it had a beginning because the laws of thermodynamics tell us that there is a limited amount of energy. No new energy is produced, and usable energy is running down. We also know it by the expanding universe. Yes, the universe is expanding. Edwin Hubble made that discovery.

Then there is the "background radiation echo." This was discovered by two Bell Laboratory Technicians in Holmdel, New Jersey. Arno Penzias and Robert Wilson were operating a huge horn antenna that mapped signals from the Milky Way when they encountered a "hum" that had them questioning. What they thought was interference was actually a measurement of heat from a great explosion; it is now called the Cosmic Microwave Radiation (CMR). Everywhere they pointed their equipment in space, they found this hum. Their citation reads that this discovery is proof that the universe began with a violent explosion. They later were awarded the Nobel Prize.

The arguments from cosmology are much more sophisticated than I've explained so far, but essentially I've demonstrated that if the universe has a beginning it has to have a cause. If it has a beginning, the cause had to produce everything in the universe. Therefore, this cause has immense power. Whatever caused it has to be outside of time, space, and matter since those were caused in the beginning of the universe.

If time began at the beginning of the universe, we can say that time was not existent before then. We also can say the same thing for space since time and space are related together. We then see that time, space, and matter all had a beginning, and therefore could not be the cause of the universe.

If the cause is outside of time, it is timeless or eternal. If it is outside of space, it is infinite. If it is apart or not material, then it is immaterial. So we could say that this cause is eternal, infinite, immaterial, and immensely powerful.

Finally, if it is true that nothing cannot produce something, then there had to be something to produce the universe. The question remains: Is the *something* a being (a person) or is it a force? These questions are answered when we consider the next arguments.

The Teleological or Design Argument

If the universe has design, it has a designer. The universe has design. The universe has a designer.

Does the universe have design or is it the product of random acts of laws? Is it the product of unguided natural selection? If it is designed, then it needs a designer. Today scientists record over 150 "just right" or anthropic principles. An anthropic principle is a principle of nature, a set law or a constant that must exist in order for life to exist on earth. Some examples are the gravitational pull of the moon on the earth's oceans, the distance of the sun to the earth, and gravity itself. Moving any of these constants would cause havoc or complete destruction on the earth. So far scientists have found over 150 of these constants, and they are still counting.

One of the strongest cases for design is information. Where did information come from? The naturalist would tell us there is no intelligence in the universe. However, information relies on intelligence. Without intelligence, information is useless and more than likely non-existent.

The naturalist would have us subscribe to the idea that there is no mind, no soul, and no spirit. My position is that if the universe has no meaning, we would never know it. Meaning assumes a mind. To say something is meaningless, I have to know what meaning is so I can contrast meaninglessness.

Consider the design of any biological cell. It requires information and the ability to process it in order to function. Biologists tell us that cells are very well designed molecular machines. Where did the original information come from? No one sees sky writing and thinks they are looking at unique cloud formations. Words spelled out in white smoke communicate a mind behind the words. Why then, when we encounter intelligent information within the cell, do we think it is the product of an unguided, purposeless engine we call natural selection?

When we look around in the natural world, we see that design is revealed everywhere. I recommend, Illustra Media's products, especially *Metamorphosis,* as a wonderful illustration of God's design. From other sources I've learned about design in the animal world in creatures like the red headed woodpecker, the giraffe, and others. It's hard to think that natural selection made these creatures evolve slowly over long, unguided periods of time.

ID and the Design Argument

Intelligent Design (ID) is a fascinating movement. It is almost always mistaken for a Christian argument for Creation. However, ID simply makes the claim that there are patterns in nature best explained by an intelligence. Nowhere in ID literature is the Christian God or any god presented as the cause or the source of this intelligence. However, the Christian apologist would be mistaken not to learn about ID.

The *Discovery Institute*[30] is the place to go to read the articles, blogs, and get resources concerning intelligent design. William Dembski, Michael Behe, Stephen Meyer, and Jonathan Wells are but a few of the scholars involved with Discovery Institute. It is worth the time to do some heavy lifting in this area.

The Moral Argument

The Moral Argument goes like this: If a moral law exists, there is a moral law giver.

There is a moral law. Therefore there is a moral law giver.

Morality describes right and wrong behavior. Ethics prescribe how we ought to live, and morality describes how we are living. In this sense, this ought to be the "ethical argument," too. As we look at similarities in cultures around the world, we notice that people everywhere have a sense of right and wrong behavior. For instance, people know it is wrong to intentionally take the life of an innocent human being, especially a child. We know it is wrong to take the property of someone else without their consent. It is wrong to take another's wife, and certainly no one likes to be lied to. Perhaps this is the point to be made. We may think we are relativists when it comes to morals—until someone does something morally wrong to us.

The point is that objective morals exist. If there is only one objective moral in the world, we have to ask where it came from. In other words, if there is a moral code there must be a code giver. This is not to question whether people can be good without God. Of course they can. This is not the issue at all. Certainly people can have good behavior, act courageously, and be self-sacrificing without God. The point is: How do we know it is good behavior, and why would we think that self-sacrificing is a good thing to do? This does not fit with the Darwinist survival of the fittest or self-preservation ideals.

The concept of *good* itself is foundational in this argument. Where do we get the idea of good? We have to admit that it is religious or moral. As C. S. Lewis has said,

> *Think of a country where people were admired for running away in battle, or where a man felt proud of double-crossing all the people who had been kindest to him. You might just as well try to imagine a country where two and two made five. Men have differed as regards what people you ought to be unselfish to—whether it was only your own family, or your fellow countrymen, or every one. But they have always agreed that you ought not to put yourself first. Selfishness has never been admired.*[31]

Why is that? Where did we get the idea that running away in a battle is a bad thing?

This morality is extreme or absolute. It is never right to torture babies for fun. It is never right to intentionally take the life of an innocent human being or steal from someone. Therefore, there is a moral code that can be found in every corner of the earth. A question comes with this: Can people suppress this code or alter it? Yes, they can. They can decide it is correct to take the life of their enemy or take the enemy's goods. The law can be twisted to fit a culture's desires. That doesn't make it go away. The law of gravity can be overcome, but not sustained without continuous attention.

In conclusion, if there is a moral code then there is a moral code giver. If there is a moral law there is a moral law giver. This precludes this from being simply a force because only persons promote morality, at least those we know of. Being a moral law giver is a personal trait.

What have we discovered from these arguments? From the cosmological arguments we find that there is an eternal, infinite, spiritual being who is immensely powerful, and who caused the universe to exist. From the teleological or design argument, we find that this being is highly intelligent and purposed a specific order in what is created. From the moral argument, we discover that this being is a personal being with the sense of absolute right and wrong behavior.

The cumulative result of these arguments demonstrates a "Being" who is best revealed as the God of the Bible. Although these arguments are in an elementary form, they lay the groundwork for acknowledging God's existence. When you have cause, design, and morality you have a highly personal, extremely intelligent, and powerful Being.

Chapter Eleven

THE PROBLEM OF EVIL

In the last chapter, we looked at arguments for the existence of God. The problem of evil is an argument that tries to disprove His existence. We all know of examples of senseless evil. As I write this, I have recently watched the news describe the senseless murder of twenty innocent school children at Sandy Hook Elementary School. We have also been recently shocked by the terrorist bombing at the Boston Marathon. Some question how God could allow these things to happen. In the minds of many, God is somehow responsible.

The fact that God is maligned today shows how our worldview has changed. For many, it is God who is brought to trial and charged with various offenses. The offense I will cover in this chapter is: Why does God allow evil to exist? Another way to state it is: Why does God allow bad things to happen to good people? People argue, "If God is all powerful and if God is all good, He would not allow evil to exist. So because evil exists, it means that God does not exist or that God is not all powerful or that He is not all good."

The argument could be stated like this:

An all-loving, all-powerful God would not allow evil to exist.

Evil exists. Therefore, an all-loving, all-powerful God does not exist.

The assumption of this argument against God is that an all powerful, all good God cannot coexist with evil. It is a hidden assumption, but an assumption nonetheless. Where does it say that God wouldn't allow evil to exist? Perhaps this is where unsound reasoning gets the best of people. Is it impossible for God to coexist with evil? Are they saying it is implausible or improbable for God to coexist with evil? The intellectual objection is: "I think it is irrational that God would permit evil." The emotional objection is: "I don't like a God who would permit evil."

The other assumption is that evil and suffering are interchangeable terms. Although the argument against God does not state suffering, the one statement does imply it. "If God is all powerful and if God is all good, He would not allow bad things to happen to good people." This causes us to ask whether all suffering is equal, and whether God is responsible for all human suffering because He allows it under His watch.

There are other assumptions here, too. One assumption is that God micro-manages all things, and that human free will is not responsible. To be sure, it is the Christian who must answer these questions. The atheist has no response except "stuff happens." Atheists can't answer *why* things happen just that they do. They can describe the shifting of tectonic plates that cause earthquakes, but that would be the limit of their explanation. Conversely, Hindus do not believe evil exists, but that it is an illusion. If God is everything and everything is God (as Hindus believe), evil cannot exist.

So how does the Christian respond? First, we must clarify that not all suffering is evil. Evil can cause suffering, but is not an interchangeable concept. I suffer when I go to the dentist, but the outcome is good and not evil. The dentist's drill is not evil even though it may cause me to suffer. It's too simplistic to think all suffering is caused by evil.

The poor suffer and sometimes it is at the hands of evil, greedy people. Sometimes it is because they are lazy or have made stupid mistakes. As I have said, not all suffering is equal, and it certainly cannot be equated with evil. For this reason, I will discuss them separately in order to provide basic answers to the questions above about the problem of evil.

Evil

First, let's talk about evil. The primary question is, How did evil get here? If God created everything, why did He create evil? The answer is found in the concept of a *thing*. Did God create everything? Yes, but is evil a *thing*? Evil is not a substance or a thing, but the *absence* of something. Where good should exist but does not, this is evil. Anything that opposes the will of God is evil. Any action that opposes God is evil, no matter the intention.

Saint Augustine gave the analogy of blindness, stating that where sight ought to exist but doesn't is evil. This is true only when there should be a seeing eye. Rocks don't have eyes, and therefore they do not see. We could say they're blind, but this isn't evil because rocks are not supposed to see. Evil is like rust on iron or steel. Rust is the corruption of these metals. You never find a pile of rust without it being attached to iron or steel.

Dr. Geisler would use the illustration of a moth-eaten garment like a sweater. The holes represent evil. We will never see a completely moth-eaten garment; all we would see is a hanger! In the same way, evil does not exist without some good to corrupt. It is a privation as in deprivation. It deprives the good iron with its corruption.

How did evil get here? We can trace it back to Adam and his freedom to choose God. His freedom to choose

God is what we term *free will*. We know from the biblical record that Adam did not choose to obey God. Some might ask, "Did free will cause evil?" Free will did not cause evil, but the *possibility* of evil. Free will is not evil, but it must exist because freedom to choose is part of our humanity.

Why did God allow free will if He knew people would choose evil? To answer this question we must ask another question: Can love be true or real without free will? If God made us love Him, would that be love? Obviously, the answer to that is, "No." Thus, the creation of humanity with a free will was the best way to enable people to freely choose God. Yes, there was a chance that people would (and will) choose wrongly, but even when they do it is not the end of the story.

Before this, Satan had to choose between serving God or himself. Obviously he chose himself. This was the real beginning of evil.

As in the previous chapter these responses are simple, but the essence of the answers is real and strong. Many books on apologetics explain the complex answers in a very convincing and detailed way. This is just a primer to get you started.

Suffering

Now that we've covered the origin of evil, let's talk about suffering. Suffering is sometimes caused by evil. People choose to act in evil ways and cause others to suffer. This is true. We see the height of evil when people have power to hurt and deprive others of their God-given identity. Injustice is evil because justice is good. Where justice ought to be exercised, but injustice prevails, this is evil.

So it is not impossible for God and evil to coexist. Neither is it unreasonable or implausible. For people to be free, they must have real choice. However, people's choices are not the end of the story. Neither is this world the end of all worlds. Although this may not be the best possible world, it may be the best way to the best possible world.

It is unreasonable to think that because God has not dealt with evil, He will never deal with evil. Just because it exists now doesn't mean it will always exist. It is plausible, reasonable, and probable that God will judge evil and that righteousness will prevail. This is the philosophical side of this problem.

The biblical side tells us that God has dealt with evil by facing it Himself in the person of Jesus Christ. The Word of God became flesh and dwelt among us. He took the suffering due to all people and paid for their sin. Proving His work in the atonement, God raised Jesus from the dead, never more to be subject to death. The scriptures tells us that there is a day when all people will be judged by God, and that Jesus has made a way for us out of this judgment (see Acts 17:30-31).

These are solid answers to the dilemma of evil. When we say something like, "Just because we don't see a good reason doesn't mean it doesn't exist," to someone who doesn't believe in an all-knowing God sounds like a cop-out. But it isn't. However, even Darwinists will say they don't know everything. Therefore, we can say that the fact that we don't know the answer doesn't mean the answer doesn't exist. Often Darwinists accuse Christians of using this "God of the gaps" excuse. Whenever we don't know the answer, we simply inject God. It is true that this can be a ploy, but it is not so in this case.

No one knows the end from the beginning—that is, unless there is a God who does. It is true that none of us see things completely correctly—unless there is an all-knowing God. It is unfair of the atheist to ask us to explain why evil exists, and then not accept our presuppositions for the existence of an all-powerful (omnipotent), all-knowing (omniscient), and all-good (omnibenevolent) God. The reality is God does not reveal everything to us. As the Bible says, "The secret things belong to the Lord our God but to us and to our children the things that are revealed" (Deuteronomy 29:29).[32]

Conclusion

Congratulations! You've traversed some new territory, and learned some new things. You are on your way to a viable understanding of apologetics so that you may defend the faith in our modern culture.

Perspective is very important. Vacation brochures try to give you a sense of where you are going to travel, and what may be available for you to experience. They want to give a perspective that could orient you to this place.

Another way to illustrate this is what happens when you join a gym. This book is like having someone give you the tour. A staff person shows you the equipment, the locker rooms, and explains the hours of operation, but you still have to go back and workout. Now you know what using the tool of apologetics basically entails. Now it is your responsibility to go to the resources, and begin to do your own heavy lifting.

I've placed a priority on truth, its concept and content. Knowing the difference between the two will help you assess arguments as well as establish your belief system. Promoting truth by stating its obvious presence and necessity for competing in the battle for ideas will help you when you engage in arguments.

What I've also attempted to do in this book is to state some obvious (and perhaps some not so obvious) things related to apologetics. I haven't covered everything on the subject, but have laid out the necessities, given a

Scriptural foundation, and presented some ways apologetics are used in the Scripture. Hopefully, this has built your confidence.

Knowing you need to be ready, that you are in a fight, the kinds of weapons needed for this fight, and how to use them is crucial to being an overcomer and winning someone to Jesus.

Finally, I presented the basic arguments for the existence of God, and an introduction to the problem of evil. These answers may seem more complicated and involved, but the reality is that the majority of people you will engage will not know most of what I have given you here. There is much more to the cosmological argument. However, this is for you to pursue. The same is true for the teleological or the argument for design. As new forms of arguments have surfaced, new challenges to the arguments have been presented. However, the basic understanding of the arguments remains the same.

Even the moral argument is under fire. New challenges to the argument have been presented and made the Christian apologist think critically about the challenge and find adequate responses. This is basically how it works with the battle for ideas. Referring back to truth as the first point, we know that truth will always prevail. Truth will always lead us to the correct response and more than adequate answer. The Holy Spirit will help you as you study and research; He will guide you to the right answers.

A final illustration may help you pursue apologetics, and even better, become engaged in the conversation about the unique truthfulness of the gospel of Jesus Christ.

My vocation in the U.S. Air Force was officially as a "crash rescue-man." If you have ever seen the guys in cumbersome silver-colored suits dragging fire hoses and spreading foam as they approach a burning aircraft, you know what I did. Admittedly, I would break into a sweat thinking about walking among the flames. The objective was to cut a path through the flames, laying down a blanket of foam to approach the aircraft. Fortunately, a rather large "crash rescue" truck had a water cannon that knocked down the flames. That's when our part came. We would literally have to walk through the fire. Usually part of a two-man team, we would drag the heavy hose while wearing a fifty-pound suit.

During our training, hundreds of gallons of jet fuel would be spread around the shell of an old aircraft and then lit. The "whoosh" of the igniting flames signaled time to get into it. The truck would use its water cannon to begin an initial path; then the lineman would have to make their way to the aircraft.

McGuire Air Force Base in New Jersey was one of the busiest in the world. Training was crucial. Every week or so we would have these practice drills at all times of the day or night. The drill times were not announced to us—to give it as realistic a feel as possible. We would receive an unexpected call, load up the trucks, and race for the flames. The truck drivers would operate the water cannon, and the crew would use the hose lines, working our way to the downed aircraft, and rescuing personnel trapped inside. We literally walked through the fire.

The illustration serves to explain something about apologetics. The professional apologists are the ones who do the work of cutting the path. They are the heavy weights. The "rest of us" are the ones who are on the ground encountering conversations every day. In reality, we are not going to discover new arguments, but the professionals will. We'll walk on the paths they make getting to whoever is "trapped" in the plane. Our job is to know the arguments—to know where it is safe to walk, and use the work of others to reach those who are trapped in false ideologies.

It is now up to you to pursue these subjects farther. Go ahead. Dive in deep and do the heavy lifting. You won't regret it!

RECOMMENDED RESOURCES

Apologetics for the Twenty-First Century, **Louis Markos**

Conviction Without Compromise: Standing Strong in the Core Beliefs of the Christian Faith, **Norman Geisler and Ron Rhodes**

Holman Quick Source Guide to Christian Apologetics, **Doug Powell**

I Don't Have Enough Faith To Be An Atheist, **Norman L. Geisler and Frank Turek.**

Is God a Moral Monster: Making Sense of the Old Testament God, **Paul Copan**

Mere Christianity, **C. S. Lewis**

Relativism: Feet Firmly Planted in Mid-Air, **Francis J. Beckwith and Gregory Koukl**

Tactics: A Game Plan for Discussing Your Christian Convictions, **Gregory Koukl**

The Abolition of Man, **C. S. Lewis**

The Apologetics of Jesus: A Caring Approach to Dealing with Doubters, **Norman L. Geisler and Patrick Zukerian**

The Big Book of Christian Apologetics: An A to Z Guide, **Norman L. Geisler**

The Case for a Creator, **Lee Strobel**

The Case for the Resurrection of Jesus, **Gary Habermas and Mike Licona**

Thinking about Christian Apologetics: What It Is and Why We Do It, **James K. Beilby**

True for You but Not for Me: Overcoming Objections to Christian Faith, **Paul Copan**

Truth Decay: Defending Christianity Against the Challenges of Postmodernism, **Douglas Groothuis**

When God Goes to Starbucks: A Guide for Everyday Apologetics, **Paul Copan**

Videos

Metamorphosis (Illustria Media)

The Case for Christ's Resurrection DVD

The Exodus Revealed: Searching for the Red Sea Crossing DVD

The Lee Strobel 3-Disc Film Collection: The Case for Christ, The Case for Faith, The Case for Creation

True U (especially for high school and college students)

YouTube

For the best results, go to www.YouTube.com or www. Vimeo.com and search for the names of people such as:

William Lane Craig

Ravi Zacharias

Gary Habermas

Norman L. Geisler

John Lennox (one of my favorites)

J. P. Moreland

Frank Turek

These are just a few to get you started.

Endnotes

Introduction

1. Neo-Darwinism has mixed the Darwinian belief in natural selection with eugenics.

2. Several articles cover this well: Cornelius Hunter, "Evolution Is Crumbling" (April 24, 2004); http://darwins-god.blogspot.com/2012/04/evolution-is-crumbling-and-now-even.html (accessed April 25, 2013); David Berlinski, "The Deniable Darwin," *Commentary*, 101.6 (June 1996); http://www.arn.org/docs/berlinski/db_deniabledarwin0696.htm (accessed April 25, 2013); Manjir Samantha-Laughton, "Dawkins, Darwin, and Other Dogma: How the Tenants of Biology Are Crumbling," *Noetic Now Journal* (Dec 2010); http://noetic.org/noetic/issue-five-december/dawkins-darwin-and-other-dogma-how-the-tenets-of-b/ (accessed April 25, 2013); See also Phillip E. Johnson, *The Wedge of Truth* (Downers Grove, IL: IVP, 2002).

3. "Evolutionary Psychology Teaches Rape 101," *Slate* (Jan. 13, 2000); http://www.slate.com/articles/news_and_politics/culturebox/2000/01/evolutionary_psychology_teaches_rape_101.html (accessed April 15, 2013). See also the Discovery Institute at www.discovery.org.

4. "Remember serial killer Jeffrey Dahmer? Darwinism played a role in his crimes too," *Uncommon Descent* (June 28, 2012); http://www.uncommondescent.com/darwinism/remember-serial-killer-jeffrey-dahmer-darwinism-played-a-role-in-his-crimes-too/ (accessed April 25, 2013).

Chapter One

5. The authority of Holy Scripture, faith, grace, the oneness of God, the Trinity, the deity of Christ, His virgin birth, His vicarious death and bodily resurrection, His ascension and His promise to return are the basic essentials of evangelical Christianity.

6. Doug Powell, *Holman Quick Source Guide to Christian Apologetics,* Kindle Edition (Nashville, TN: B&H Publishing Group, 2006), 370–371.

7. We frame an argument when we determine what the main point (thesis) of the argument will be and then keep the discussion clearly on topic. We define the terms and ask questions when points are made. We also deflect irrelevant points and point back to the thesis.

8. Jay Heinrichs, *Thank You for Arguing: What Aristotle, Lincoln, and Homer Simpson Can Teach Us About the Art of Persuasion,* Kindle Edition (New York: Random House, 2008), 164–168.

Chapter Two

9. Craig S. Keener, *The IVP Bible Background Commentary: New Testament* (Downers Grove, IL: InterVarsity Press, 1993), Romans 1:19–22.

10. Patrick Zukeran and Norman Geisler, *The Apologetics of Jesus: A Caring Approach to Dealing with Doubters,* Kindle Edition (Ada, MI: Baker Books, 2009), 32–34.

Chapter Three

11. Norman L. Geisler and Frank Turek, *I Don't Have Enough Faith to Be an Atheist* (Wheaton, IL: Crossway, 2004).

12. Douglas Groothuis, *Truth Decay: Defending Christianity Against the Challenges of Postmodernism,* Kindle Edition (Downers Grove, IL: InterVarsity Press, 2000), 59–61.

Chapter Four

13. Craig S. Keener, *The IVP Bible Background Commentary: New Testament* (Downers Grove, IL: InterVarsity Press, 1993), 2 Corinthians 10:3–5.

14. Gregory Bassham, William Irwin, Henry Nardone, and James M. Wallace, *Critical Thinking: A Student's Introduction,* Kindle Edition (New York: McGraw-Hill, 2002), 1.

15. Denyse O'Leary, *By Design or by Chance? The Growing Controversy on the Origins of Life in the Universe,* Kindle Edition (Minneapolis, MN: Augsburg Fortress, 2004), 487–489.

16. Norman L. Geisler, *Baker Encyclopedia of Christian Apologetics,* Kindle Edition (Ada, MI: Baker Academic, 1998), 35094–35096.

17. John Godfrey Saxe, "Blind Men and the Elephant" (1816-1887), poem based on an ancient Indian fable. Accessed at www.allaboutphilosophy.org/blind-men-and-the-elephant.htm.

18. For more along these lines, see Geisler and Turek, *I Don't Have Enough Faith To Be An Atheist.*

Chapter Six

19. Charles Swindoll, "No Time to Remain Silent," (2009) *Insight for Living, Canada;* http://www.

insightforliving.ca/insights/february-2009/no-time-remain-silent.html (accessed April 5, 2013).

20. Norman Geisler and Ron Rhodes, *Conviction Without Compromise: Standing Strong in the Core Beliefs of the Christian Faith* (Eugene, OR: Harvest House, 2008).

21. For more information, visit www.ratiochristi.org.

22. Albert Mohler, "'You Are Bringing Strange Things to Our Ears': Christian Apologetics for a Postmodern Age," *RobertMohler.com* (Oct. 10, 2005); http://www.albertmohler.com/2005/10/10/you-are-bringing-strange-things-to-our-ears-christian-apologetics-for-a-postmodern-age-2/ (accessed April 11, 2013).

Chapter Seven

23. For a more thorough teaching on the Unknown God, see *Eternity in Their Hearts* by Don Richardson (Ventura, CA: Regal, 2006).

24. Doug Powell, *Holman QuickSource Guide to Christian Apologetics,* Kindle Edition (Nashville, TN: B

Chapter Eight

25. Doug Powell, *Holman QuickSource Guide to Christian Apologetics,* Kindle Edition (Nashville, TN: B&H Publishing Group, 2006), 370–371.

26. http://blog.acton.org/archives/1863-college-professors-biased-against-christians.html

Chapter Nine

27. After this, I was pleasantly surprised to find a book that had basically done the same thing, only they had found three. *Making Sense of Your World: A Biblical Worldview* by W. Gary Phillips, William E. Brown, and John Stonestreet (Salem, WI: Sheffield, 2008).

28. This is epistemology or the study of how we know what we know.

Chapter Ten

29. Norman L. Geisler, *Baker Encyclopedia of Christian Apologetics,* Kindle Edition (Ada, MI: Baker Academic, 1998), 121.
30. For more information on ID visit www.discovery.org.
31. C. S. Lewis, *Mere Christianity,* Kindle Edition (New York: HarperCollins, 2009), 294–297.

Chapter Eleven

32. What about "cult apologetics"? How do we witness to or debate with a Muslim? In this book, I have not presented or described how to engage cults (any off-shoot of a mainline religion) or other world religions. To cover these subjects adequately, I would need to write another book or two. I have listed some excellent resources on how to engage cults at the end of this book. As far as world religions go, Dr. Win Corduan has written what I believe is the best book on world religions, *Neighboring Faiths.* You would do well to read this to gain an understanding of the major religions of the world and how and why they differ with Christianity. Admittedly, I have attempted to not overload the reader with too much information, so I've left a fair bit up to you, the reader, to pursue in your own studies.

ABOUT RAY CIERVO

Ray Ciervo is the founder of Ray Ciervo Ministries, an apologetic ministry geared to equip the Church for its work of service. Although the study of apologetics is normally viewed (and presented) as a "heady" subject, Ray makes it practical and usable for the Church's work in evangelism and spiritual growth. Ray conducts seminars, conferences, and classes on subjects including building a biblical worldview, the existence of God, Intelligent Design, creation vs. evolution, world religions, the reliability of the Bible, moral relativism, and the necessity of truth. In all his teaching, Ray focuses on showing the historical evidence for the resurrection of Jesus Christ, God's Son.

Ray also teaches the Church the basics of Christian conduct, character, leadership, and servanthood. Knowledge of the Scripture and years of experience give Ray a platform to speak on subjects that help to keep the Church focused on its mission. Ray has ministered in a variety of positions—from pastoring to church planting, training leaders, and teaching as an adjunct professor in Bible College. Ray received his master's degree in apologetics from Southern Evangelical Seminary (SES) in 2002 (*summa cum laude*). He is actively pursuing his doctor of ministry also from SES.

Ray has also traveled extensively in England and South America for almost forty years. In the past few years, Ray has traveled to South Africa, Greece, Italy, and Macedonia as well, teaching and preaching on apologetics and Christian worldview.

What drives Ray is his love for God, the Scripture, and the Church. He continually strives to equip the Church with tools to remain faithful to the Scripture and relevant to the world.

Ray is married to Joanne and presently lives in Eatontown, New Jersey. They have three children, seven grandchildren, and one great-granddaughter.

Ray is available to speak at your church or conference, hold seminars or help put on a conference.

Please contact Ray at "info@nopatanswers.com or (888) 264-3979 if you would like to book him for meetings.

Also visit Ray's website: www.nopatanswers.com for videos and articles.

CPSIA information can be obtained at www.ICGtesting.com
Printed in the USA
BVOW04s0809130813

328436BV00002B/5/P